Performing Arts

**Titles in the
Discovering Careers
series**

Adventure
Animals
Art
Computers
Construction
Environment
Fashion
Food
Health
Math
Movies
Nature
Performing Arts
Science
Space Exploration
Sports
Transportation
Writing

Performing Arts

Ferguson's

An Infobase Learning Company

Discovering Careers: Performing Arts

Ferguson's
An imprint of Infobase Learning
132 West 31st Street
New York NY 10001

Library of Congress Cataloging-in-Publication Data

Performing arts.
    p. cm. — (Discovering careers)
  Includes bibliographical references and index.
  ISBN-13: 978-0-8160-8059-5 (hardcover : alk. paper)
  ISBN-10: 0-8160-8059-3 (hardcover : alk. paper) 1. Performing arts—Vocational guidance—Juvenile literature. I. Ferguson Publishing.
  PN1580.P42 2011
  790.2023—dc23   2011023748

Ferguson's books are available at special discounts when purchased in bulk quantities for businesses, associations, institutions, or sales promotions. Please call our Special Sales Department in New York at (212) 967-8800 or (800) 322-8755.

You can find Ferguson's on the World Wide Web at
http://www.infobaselearning.com

Text design by Erik Lindstrom and Erika K. Arroyo
Composition by Erika K. Arroyo
Cover printed by Yurchak Printing, Landisville, Pa.
Book printed and bound by Yurchak Printing, Landisville, Pa.

Printed in the United States of America

This book is printed on acid-free paper.

CONTENTS

Introduction

You may not have decided yet what you want to be in the future. And you don't have to decide right away. You do know that right now you are interested in one or more of the performing arts. Do any of the statements below describe you? If so, you may want to begin thinking about what a career in the performing arts might mean for you.

____My favorite class in school is music.

____I enjoy performing in front of an audience.

____I take ballet/jazz/tap lessons.

____I take music lessons.

____I try out for parts in school plays.

____I sing in my school or church choir.

____I enjoy putting on plays with my friends.

____I like to make movies with my video camera.

____I listen to music whenever I can.

____I like to write plays.

____I am good at giving speeches and oral presentations.

____I play in the school band or orchestra.

____I see as many movies and plays as I can.

____I enjoy going to live music or dance concerts.

____I like to read biographies of famous performers.

Discovering Careers: Performing Arts is a book about careers in the performing arts, from actors, to musicians, to stunt performers. Performing artists include those who work in theater, film, television, radio, music, and dance. They entertain us, educate us, and help us understand different ways of thinking and feeling.

1

This book describes many possibilities for future careers in the performing arts. Read through it and see how the different careers are connected. For example, if you are interested in acting, you will want to read the chapters on Actors, Clowns, Comedians, Magicians, and Stunt Performers. If you are interested in music, you will want to read the chapters on Composers, Music Teachers, Musical Instrument Repairers, Musicians, Pop and Rock Musicians, Singers, and Songwriters. If you want to work behind the scenes, you should read the articles on Film and Television Directors, Screenwriters, Stage Production Technicians, and other careers. Go ahead and explore!

What Do Performing Artists Do?

The first section of each chapter begins with a heading such as "What Actors Do" or "What Dancers Do." It tells what it's like to work at this job. It describes typical responsibilities and assignments. You will find out about working conditions. Which performing artists work in music or television studios? Which ones work in concert halls or schools? Which ones work in locations all across the country? This section answers all these questions.

How Do I Become a Performing Artist?

The section called "Education and Training" tells you what schooling you need for employment in each job—a high school diploma, training at a junior college, a college degree, or more. It also talks about on-the-job training that you could expect to receive after you're hired, and whether or not you must complete an apprenticeship program.

How Much Do Performing Artists Earn?

The "Earnings" section gives the average salary figures for the job described in the chapter. These figures give you a general idea of how much money people with this job can make. Keep in mind that many people really earn more or less than the amounts given here because actual salaries depend on many different things, such as the size of the organization, the location of the organization, and the amount of education, training, and experience you have. Generally, but not always, bigger performing arts organizations located in major cities pay more than smaller ones in smaller cities and towns, and people with more education, training, and experience earn more. Also remember that these figures are current averages. They will probably be different by the time you are ready to enter the workforce.

What Will the Future Be Like for Performing Artists?

The "Outlook" section discusses the employment outlook for the career: whether the total number of people employed in this career will increase or decrease in the coming years and whether jobs in this field will be easy or hard to find. These predictions are based on economic conditions, the size and makeup of the population, interest in the particular area of the performing arts, and other factors. They come from the U.S. Department of Labor, professional associations, and other sources.

Keep in mind that these predictions are general statements. No one knows for sure what the future will be like. Also remember that the employment outlook is a general statement about an industry and does not necessarily apply to everyone. A determined and talented person may be able to find a job in an industry or career with the worst outlook. And a person without ambition and the proper training will find it difficult to find a job in even a booming industry or career field.

Where Can I Find More Information?

Each chapter includes a sidebar called "For More Info." It lists resources that you can contact to find out more about the field and careers in the field. You will find names, addresses, phone numbers, email addresses, and Web sites of performing arts-oriented associations and organizations.

Extras

Every chapter has a few extras. There are photos that show performing arts workers in action. There are sidebars and notes on ways to explore the field, fun facts, profiles of people in the field, and lists of Web sites and books that might be helpful. At the end of the book you will find three additional sections: "Glossary," "Browse and Learn More," and "Index." The Glossary gives brief definitions of words that relate to education, career training, or employment that you may be unfamiliar with. The Browse and Learn More section lists performing arts-related books, periodicals, and Web sites to explore. The Index includes all the job titles mentioned in the book.

It's not too soon to think about your future. We hope you discover several possible career choices. Happy hunting!

Actor

What Actors Do

Actors perform in movies, stage plays, and television, video, and radio productions. They use voice and gestures (movement of the limbs or body) to play, or portray, different characters. Actors spend a lot of time looking for available roles. They read and study the parts and then audition (try out) for casting directors, directors, and producers. In film and television, actors must also do screen tests, which are scenes recorded on film. Casting directors, producers, and directors study these screen tests to decide if the actor is the right person for the role. Once selected for a role, actors memorize their lines and rehearse with other cast members. If the production includes singing and dancing, more rehearsal time is needed. Rehearsal times are usually longer for live theater performances than for movie and television productions.

Theater actors, also known as *stage actors,* may perform the same part many times a week for weeks, months, and sometimes years. *Film actors* may spend weeks, months, and even up to a year on one production, which often takes place on location—that is, in different parts of the world. For example, a film may be shot in a desert, in a forest, in a big city, or on a film soundstage (a special building where movies are filmed). *Television actors* in a series, such as a soap opera, also may play the same role for years, generally in 13-week cycles. For these actors, however, their lines change from week to week and even from day to day, and much time is spent rehearsing new lines.

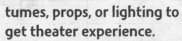

EXPLORING

- Read books about working as an actor. See the Browse and Learn More section for some suggestions.
- Visit the following Web site to learn more about a career as an actor: Acting Workshop On-Line: So You Want to be an Actor (http://www.redbird studio.com/AWOL/acting2 .html).
- Participate in school or community theater productions. You can audition for acting roles, but also work on cos-

tumes, props, or lighting to get theater experience.
- Watch as many plays, television shows, and movies as you can.
- Read biographies of famous actors and other books about acting, auditioning, theater, and the film and television industries. You can also find biographies of actors on Arts & Entertainment Network's Web site at http://www .biography.com.
- Talk to an actor about his or her career.

Stage actors perform an entire play, beginning to end, in one performance. Film and television actors usually perform scenes out of sequence during filming—they may perform the last scene first, for example. They also may have to repeat the same scene many times.

Education and Training

In high school, take as many drama classes as possible and participate in theater productions. High school and community theaters offer acting opportunities. Large cities such as New York, Chicago, and Los Angeles have public high schools for the performing arts. Special dramatic arts schools, located mainly in New York and Los Angeles, also offer training.

Although it is not required, a college education is helpful. Many aspiring actors complete at least a bachelor's degree in film, theater, or the dramatic arts. Some earn a master of fine arts degree. More than 150 programs in theater arts are accredited by the National Association of Schools of Theatre.

Helping Hands: Operation International Children

Although adults wage wars, children are typically the ones most affected. This is what Academy Award-winning actor Gary Sinise found out during a recent United Service Organizations-sponsored visit to Afghanistan and Iraq. He saw children trying to learn their lessons in makeshift school rooms, with little more than a pencil stub and used notebooks for supplies. He thought it was wrong that children did not have basic school supplies and he decided to do something about it. He teamed up with writer Laura Hillenbrand to found Operation Iraqi Children, a nonprofit, grassroots charity. To raise money, they showed people videos of Iraqi schoolchildren and spoke to many people about the need to help these kids.

Soon, school supplies poured in from many sources—schools, private donors, and large corporations. Much of the money was raised through church bake sales, school supply drives, and other community activities. Supply kits are shipped to their destinations, and handed out to Iraqi children by U.S. troops. Operation Iraqi Children has sent more than a quarter million school supply kits, and more than half a million toys to boys and girls in Iraq, Afghanistan, and other war-torn nations.

The charity recently merged with another charitable organization, People to People International, and now operates under the name, Operation International Children. Visit http://www.operationiraqichildren.org for more information.

Sources: Operation
International Children

Earnings

Most actors earned from $18,000 to $133,000 a year in 2010, according to the U.S. Department of Labor. The mean yearly salary for movie actors was $89,772. Those who worked for theater companies made $43,596.

In all areas of acting, well-known performers have salary rates above the minimums, and the salaries of the few top stars are many times higher. In movies, top stars may earn as much as $20 million per film, and, after receiving a percentage of the gross (the total earnings) earned by the film, these stars can earn far, far more.

Television and movie actors may also receive additional payments known as residuals as part of their guaranteed salary. A residual is a payment that is given to the actor whenever films or television shows in which they appear are rerun, licensed for TV exhibition, or released on DVD or online.

Outlook

There will be strong competition for acting jobs during the next decade. Many people want to become actors—especially

Screen Acting and Stage Acting

Screen acting differs from acting in a theater. In screen work, the camera can focus closely on an actor, so performances must be subtle and lifelike. Stage work requires more exaggerated gestures and speaking techniques. Movie and television actors spend a lot of time waiting for scenes to be filmed. They repeat the same scene over and over, play scenes out of order, and perform only small segments of a scene at a time. Stage actors perform an entire play at one time. Screen actors do not know how audiences react to their performance until months after they finish work on a film. Stage actors get an immediate reaction from the audience while they are performing.

FOR MORE INFO

The following is a professional union for actors in theater and "live" industrial productions.

Actors' Equity Association
165 West 46th Street
New York, NY 10036-2500
212-869-8530
http://www.actorsequity.org

For information on union representation, contact
American Federation of Television and Radio Artists
260 Madison Avenue
New York, NY 10016-2401
212-532-0800
http://www.aftra.com

For answers to a number of frequently asked questions concerning drama education, visit the NAST Web site.
National Association of Schools of Theatre (NAST)
11250 Roger Bacon Drive, Suite 21
Reston, VA 20190-5248

703-437-0700
info@arts-accredit.org
http://nast.arts-accredit.org

This union represents film and television performers. It has general information on actors, directors, and producers.
Screen Actors Guild
5757 Wilshire Boulevard, 7th Floor
Los Angeles, CA 90036-3600
323-954-1600
http://www.sag.org

For information about opportunities in nonprofit theaters, contact
Theatre Communications Group
520 Eighth Avenue, 24th Floor
New York, NY 10018-4156
212-609-5900
tcg@tcg.org
http://www.tcg.org

in the movie and television industries. In addition to film and television, there are also opportunities in theater. In the last two decades, the field has grown considerably outside New York because many major cities have started their own professional theater companies. The number of dinner theaters and summer stock companies has also increased. Cable television programming continues to add new acting opportunities, but there always will be many more actors than there are roles to play. Many actors also work as secretaries, waiters, taxi drivers, or in other jobs to earn extra income.

Choreographers

What Choreographers Do

Choreographers create original dance routines for dancers to perform. Choreographers are experts in dance and music, as well as costume, lighting, and dramatics (the art of acting). Besides inventing new dance routines, choreographers teach their dances to performers. Sometimes they direct and stage the presentation of their dances.

Choreographers sometimes specialize in one type of dance, such as ballroom, ballet, modern, jazz, acrobatic, or tap. Others use a variety of styles in one dance routine. Some choreographers create dances for dance companies to perform as part of their repertoire (a group of dances that they regularly perform). Others choreograph routines for operas, musical comedies, music videos, movies, and television productions.

Choreographers usually start out as dancers. They study dance for many years and learn all the movements and positions of the various types of dance. Each type of dance has its own movement styles and a vocabulary to describe those movements. Most basic dance movements in American dance come from ballet and use French terms, such as plié, relevé, and arabesque. Tap dance has steps called flap, shuffle, time-step, and ball-change.

Choreographers know how to use movement and music to tell a story, create a mood, express an idea, or celebrate movement itself. Since dance is so closely related to music, choreographers know about various musical styles and rhythms. They

EXPLORING

- Read books about dance and choreography. See the Browse and Learn More section for some suggestions.
- Take as many dance classes as you can. Try different types of dance.
- There are many instructional videos available that teach you ballet, tap, and ballroom dancing. It is best, though, to study with a teacher who can watch you and help you do the movements correctly, so you don't develop bad habits or injure yourself.

- Once you have learned some dance technique, begin to give recitals and performances. Performing and rehearsing will give you experience working with a choreographer.
- Try to choreograph a dance routine for a school performance or community event. Participate in any school or community stage production that has dance numbers.
- Talk to a choreographer about his or her career.

often hear a piece of music first and then choreograph a dance to it. Sometimes choreographers plan the dance, then choose the dancers and teach them movements. But most often they work with their dancers, and change the choreography to take best advantage of the dancers' abilities. Choreographers must also be flexible enough to change their dances to fit different performance spaces.

Education and Training

There are no formal educational requirements, but an early start in dance classes (around eight years old for ballet, slightly older for jazz, tap, modern, folk, or acrobatic dance) and years of practice are essential. Talented students begin serious training with regional or national dance schools in their early teens. Many dancers have professional auditions by the time they are 17 or 18 years old.

A college degree is not necessarily an advantage for professional choreographers, but there are many colleges that offer degrees in dance with choreography courses.

Earnings

Salaries depend on the size of the theater and earnings from performance royalties and fees. In small professional theaters, choreographers may earn about $1,000 per week, and

Profile: Twyla Tharp (b. 1941)

Dancer and choreographer Twyla Tharp is known for her imaginative works that combine modern and traditional dance movements. *Eight Jelly Rolls, Push Comes to Shove,* and *Bach Partita* are some of her works.

Tharp was born in Portland, Indiana, and studied music and dance as a child. While attending Barnard College in New York City, she studied dance with famous dancers and choreographers such as Merce Cunningham, Martha Graham, and others. Tharp first danced professionally with the Paul Taylor Dance Company. She formed her own company, Twyla Tharp Dance, in 1965. She also choreographed dances for the Joffrey Ballet, American Ballet Theatre, The Martha Graham Dance Company, and other dance companies. Tharp choreographed the motion pictures *Hair* (1979), *Amadeus* (1984), and *White Nights* (1985), among other movies. She directed and choreographed the Broadway musical *Singin' in the Rain.* According to her Web site, Tharp has "choreographed more than 135 dances, five Hollywood movies, and directed and choreographed four Broadway shows." Visit http://www.twylatharp.org to learn more about her career.

Source: TwylaTharp.com

FOR MORE INFO

For information on all aspects of dance, contact
American Dance Guild
240 West 14th Street
New York, NY 10011-7218
http://americandanceguild.org

For articles and press releases about dance-related topics, visit the Dance/USA Web site.
Dance/USA
1111 16th Street, NW, Suite 300
Washington, DC 20036-4830
202-833-1717
http://www.danceusa.org

For information on educational programs and a helpful FAQ section, visit

National Association of Schools of Dance (NASD)
11250 Roger Bacon Drive, Suite 21
Reston, VA 20190-5248
703-437-0700
info@arts-accredit.org
http://nasd.arts-accredit.org

For information on careers in dance, contact
National Dance Association
American Alliance for Health, Physical Education, Recreation & Dance
1900 Association Drive
Reston, VA 20191-1598
800-213-7193, ext. 464
http://www.aahperd.org/nda

---

as much as $30,000 for a Broadway (the main theater district in New York City) production requiring eight to 10 weeks of rehearsal time. When working for big-budget movies, choreographers can earn an average of $3,000 per week. Those working in television can about $10,000 in a 14-day period.

Salaried choreographers had median yearly earnings of $37,660 in 2010, according to the U.S. Department of Labor. Earnings ranged from less than $19,000 to $71,000 or more.

Tips for Success

To be a successful choreographer, you should

- love dancing
- be very creative
- be a good teacher
- have excellent communication skills
- be organized

Outlook

Employment for choreographers is expected to be fair during the next decade. Only the most talented choreographers will find jobs. Very few dancers and choreographers work year round and they often take other jobs to make extra money. More than half the dance companies in the United States are in New York City, which means the majority of choreographers live there, too. There are opportunities in other large cities where there are dance companies and theater companies. There is some work available in film, television, and music videos, too.

Circus Performers

What Circus Performers Do

Circus performers do daring and dangerous physical acts to entertain and thrill live audiences.

There are many types of circus performers. *Trapeze artists* leap from one trapeze to another, or do somersaults in midair. *Highwire* or *wire walkers* may walk, ride bicycles, unicycles, or do gymnastic moves on a wire suspended high above the ground. *Acrobats* perform gymnastic routines of many varieties. *Animal trainers* show off the strength or abilities of animals, such as elephants, lions, tigers, and horses, while often appearing to risk their own lives. *Aerialists* perform various athletic feats in the air such as flips and spins. *Jugglers* can keep many objects in the air at once. They can do this even if the objects are dangerous ones like fiery rings or knives. *Clowns* perform comedic routines. Most circuses also have a circus band whose *musicians* keep the action exciting as they play along with the various acts.

Most circuses have several circus performers working at once in different rings (areas where circus workers perform). These simultaneous performances are usually introduced by an *announcer,* known as the *ringmaster,* who calls the audience's attention to one or more rings. Although most circuses at one time were held in outdoor tents, known as big tops, most today are held in large indoor arenas.

Education and Training

Many full-time circus performers were born into circus families. Without coming from a circus family, becoming a

EXPLORING

- Go to every circus that comes to your area. Talk to the performers about their work.
- Learn to juggle, ride a unicycle, or do other stunts.
- Gymnastics teams, drama clubs, and dance troupes give you performance experience and may help you decide if you have talent for this type of work.
- Physical education classes and community athletic games and competitions provide excellent physical training.

- If you are interested in animal training, volunteer at nearby zoos or stables.
- You may wish to join an association of jugglers, unicyclists, or another specialty. They often hold festivals, events, and seminars where you can learn skills, get to know other circus performers, and perhaps find a mentor who can help you get into the field.

circus performer can be hard. Many acrobats, riders, and other circus performers learn their craft from more experienced performers.

No high school diploma or college degree is required by most circuses. A high school or college education, however, will help you manage your business affairs and develop good communication skills. Athletic training that develops coordination, strength, and balance is necessary for almost all circus performers. Other training includes acting, music, dance and, for those interested in animals, veterinary care. Knowledge of foreign languages will be helpful for performers who travel to countries where English is not spoken.

An acrobat swings high above the audience during a performance. (Jerret Raffety, AP Photo/*Rawlins Daily Times*)

Earnings

Circus performers just starting out usually do not earn much more than the minimum wage ($7.25 per hour), and sometimes even lower, perhaps $200 to $400 per week. Performers usually receive food and lodging. Less-skilled performers earn $600 to $700 per week, while those who work with animals earn from several thousand per week up to $100,000 or more for the circus season. Performers who develop highly unusual acts and achieve fame or recognition earn the best salaries.

DID YOU KNOW?

Where Circus Performers Work

Most circus performers are employed by traveling or resident circuses, but their skills and training also allow them to work for the following employers:

- Amusement parks
- Casinos
- Cruise lines
- Film and television industry
- Nightclubs
- Self-employment

Outlook

Circus performing is not usually permanent, full-time work. Many people have second jobs outside the circus industry. The outlook for circus performers does not seem to be improving. Those who work in a resident company of a circus can become well known and have greater job security. There are more opportunities for circus performers outside the circus, and there is always an interest in new, unusual, never-been-seen acts. The private party business is growing. Circus performers can also find work in television and performing in music videos.

Circuses have changed in recent years. Fewer circuses use live animals and the trend is toward more theatrical, themed productions. Even with the changes, circuses still remain popular. But the number of circus performers is far larger than the number of job openings.

Circus Elephants

Traditionally, a popular measure of a circus's size was the number of its elephants. Elephants hauled materials, pushed wagons, and were the big attractions in trained animal acts and in the menagerie. Today, Ringling Bros. has a large collection of Asian elephants, including those that perform with the Greatest Show on Earth and those at Ringling Bros. and Barnum & Bailey Center for Elephant Conservation. The 200-acre center was established in central Florida in 1995 to preserve the endangered Asian elephant species. Fewer than 35,000 presently remain on earth. Visit http://www.elephantcenter.com to learn more about the center.

FOR MORE INFO

This labor union serves singers, dancers, variety performers, circus performers, ice skaters, and theme park performers. It fights for better wages and offers resource information to those starting out.

American Guild of Variety Artists
363 Seventh Avenue, 17th Floor
New York, NY 10001-3904
212-675-1003
agva@agvausa.com
http://www.agvausa.com

This Web site includes information on treatment of circus animals, membership, and links to circus-related sites.

Circus Fans Association of America
http://www.circusfans.org

This circus travels across the country providing education programs to schools, businesses, and other groups. Visit its Web site to find out where the troupe is now and the programs offered.

Circus of the Kids
9042 Shoal Creek Drive
Tallahassee, FL 32312-4076
866-247-2875
http://www.circusofthekids.com

For information on performance schedules and the history of circuses, visit the Circus World Web site.

Circus World
550 Water Street
Baraboo, WI 53913-2578
866-693-1500
ringmaster@circusworldmuseum.com
http://circusworld.wisconsinhistory.org

For information on a career as a clown, contact
Clowns of America International
PO Box 1171
Englewood FL 34295-1171
877-816-6941
http://www.coai.org

For information about a career as a juggler, contact
International Jugglers' Association
PO Box 580005
Kissimmee, FL 34758-0001
http://www.juggle.org

This Web site offers facts and information about Ringling Brothers and Barnum & Bailey Circus, including news, games, animals, history and tradition, performers, and show dates.

Ringling Brothers and Barnum & Bailey
http://www.ringling.com

EXPLORING

- Try to make your friends laugh by telling jokes, coming up with funny routines, or just acting silly.
- Dress up as a clown for Halloween.
- Perform in school or community plays.
- Take classes in dance, acting (especially improvisation), mime, or gymnastics. You may find a studio or gym in your area that offers classes in juggling, trampoline, acrobatics, magic, or other skills useful for clowns.
- Volunteer to perform as a clown for hospitals, parades, or charitable events.
- Check your library for books about clowning and clown history.
- Talk to a clown about his or her career.

What Clowns Do

Clowns work in circuses, in movies, on television, in musical plays, at birthday parties and other events, or in fairgrounds or amusement parks. They perform comical routines often while wearing unusual makeup and costumes. They juggle, dance, ride unicycles, walk tightropes, or perform other tricks and skills to make people laugh.

Circus clowns often perform routines to entertain audiences while other acts are being set up. They sing songs, tell jokes, or do acrobatic stunts. Clowns have a good sense of timing and balance. They are able to improvise, or make things up on the spot. Every audience is different and clowns change their performances according to how the audience reacts.

The makeup and costumes vary for different kinds of clowns. *White-face clowns* wear white makeup and caps that make them appear to be bald. They are the elegant clowns and are often in charge of a routine.

Auguste clowns wear baggy clothes and act clumsy or silly. They trip over objects on the stage or drop things other clowns are juggling. *Tramp clowns* wear tattered clothes and are sad or forlorn. *Character clowns* have unique routines, and usually perform alone.

Clowns usually have to travel to find work. For jobs with traveling circuses, they travel for much of the year. Circus clowns may perform in a large tent outdoors or in a large indoor

Clown hopefuls audition at the Ringling Brothers Barnum & Bailey Circus Clown College. (Kathy Willens, AP Photo)

DID YOU KNOW?

Clowns have been called pranksters, mirthmakers, jesters, comics, jokers, buffoons, harlequins, fools, merry-andrews, mimes, and joeys.

Early Egyptian, Greek, and Roman rulers kept fools for entertainment. During the Middle Ages and the Renaissance, court jesters were hired for their musical and juggling skills and verbal wit. They wore colorful clothing: big collars, bells, pointed caps, and unusual shoes. Many jesters were traveling minstrels, skilled in storytelling, juggling, singing, magic, tightrope walking, and acrobatics.

After the Renaissance, clowns became stage characters, such as country bumpkins or dim-witted servants. The word *clown* was first used in 16th-century England to describe a clumsy, country oaf. Small traveling street theaters used them to attract audiences to their plays.

arena. Those who work at fairs or amusement parks usually perform outdoors, wandering the grounds, gathering audiences in various locations.

Education and Training

A high school diploma is not required by most circuses, but a diploma and a college education will help your job prospects. Employers in the movie and television industries also prefer to hire performers who have diplomas.

Clowns need to move well and use their bodies to communicate with audiences. Training in dance and pantomime (communicating by using facial expressions and other movements) is helpful. Dance academies and schools for dramatic arts offer classes in pantomime and dance. Many high schools also have drama or dance classes for students.

Clowns should be able to project their voices, or make them heard easily by audiences. Any debate or public speaking clubs can help develop this skill. Clowns need to have good voice control as well as poise (the ability to not get nervous or flustered) before an audience. Participating in school or community plays is good training.

Earnings

There are no set salaries for clowns. Circus clowns earn about $400 to $500 per week. Those who work in nightclubs, casinos, or on Broadway (the main theater district in New York City) can make as much as $10,000, according to the American Guild of Variety Artists. Weekly income can vary widely—clowns may earn $300 one week, $1,000 the next, and nothing the week after that. For a child's birthday party, a clown earns $50 to $500 depending on the length of the party and the performer's popularity.

Words to Learn

alley a circus term for the area that the clowns use for makeup and costume changes; the term, **clown alley**, now refers to clown groups, clubs, or troupes

blow-off a funny or surprise ending to a clown skit

bump a nose a phrase that means "good luck," similar to saying "break a leg" to an actor about to go on stage

double take showing surprise or shock at something; the clown looks, looks away, then quickly looks back again

first of May a beginner clown; traditionally a new clown has his or her first performance when the winter weather is over, usu-ally around the first of May (see plunge).

hey rube clowns yell, "hey rube," to show they are in some kind of trouble and signal other per-formers to come to the rescue

joey a clown with at least five years of experience

patter the story or script that goes along with a stunt, a comic skit, or a ventriloquist's act

plunge the first time a new clown performs in public as a clown (see first of May)

ventriloquist a performer who projects his or her voice into a wooden dummy to make it appear that the dummy is actu-ally speaking

FOR MORE INFO

This labor union serves singers, dancers, variety performers, circus performers, ice skaters, and theme park performers. It fights for better wages and offers information to those starting out.
American Guild of Variety Artists
363 Seventh Avenue, 17th Floor
New York, NY 10001-3904
212-675-1003
agva@agvausa.com
http://www.agvausa.com

This Web site includes information on treatment of circus animals, membership, and links to circus-related sites.
Circus Fans Association of America
http://www.circusfans.org

To learn more about circuses of the past as well as the present, visit the Circus World museum. If you can't make it in person, check out its Web site.
Circus World
550 Water Street
Baraboo, WI 53913-2578

866-693-1500
ringmaster@circusworldmuseum.com
http://circusworld.wisconsinhistory.org

For information about a career as a clown, contact
Clowns of America, International
PO Box 1171
Englewood, FL 34295-1171
877-816-6941
http://www.coai.org

For information about a career as a juggler, contact
International Jugglers' Association
PO Box 580005
Kissimmee, FL 34758-0001
http://www.juggle.org

This Web site offers facts and information about Ringling Brothers and Barnum & Bailey Circus, including news, games, animals, history and tradition, performers, and show dates.
Ringling Brothers and Barnum & Bailey
http://www.ringling.com

Outlook

The employment outlook for clowns is not very promising. Many people want to work as clowns. It can take a long time to find a job as a clown. Most clowns are not permanently employed and must repeatedly try out, or audition, for positions. They usually hold other jobs while they search for clowning opportunities. Many clowns volunteer to entertain at hospitals or charitable events. Volunteering is good experience and can lead to paying jobs.

Comedians

What Comedians Do

Comedians try to make people laugh. Some entertain audiences in nightclubs and at concerts. Some perform in comedy shows on television. Some work behind the scenes writing jokes, sketches, and screenplays for other comedians and actors.

Comedians who perform alone on stage are called *stand-up comedians.* They entertain audiences with stories, jokes, one-liners, and impressions. In comedy clubs in large cities, comedians may do more than one show a night. Each performance can last anywhere from 10 minutes to an hour.

Stand-up comedians travel from city to city entertaining different types of audiences. They change their routines to appeal to different groups of people. To arrange out-of-town performances, comedians may call the club owners themselves or hire a booking agent. In medium- and small-sized cities comedians may give only one performance and then drive or fly to the next city. Stand-up comedians also entertain at conventions, concerts, hotels, parties, and outdoor festivals.

Some comedians perform as members of an improvisational group, such as Second City or NBC's *Saturday Night Live.* They perform skits, dances, and musical numbers, often making up their own dialogue on the spot.

Only the best comedians appear on television and in movies. They have worked for many years developing their routines and sharpening their skills. Their popularity is the result of hard work, performing experience, and persistence. Comedians

EXPLORING

- Try your hand at comedy by acting out the scenes in the following book: *Sixty Comedy Duet Scenes for Teens: Real-Life Situations for Laughter,* by Laurie Allen (Meriwether Publishing, 2008).
- Many improvisational groups offer classes in acting and performance techniques. These groups are often highly competitive, but they are a good place to learn skills, make contacts, and have fun.
- Before you get on stage to perform for strangers, try performing for family and friends.
- Most comedy clubs and coffee houses have open mike nights where aspiring comedians can get on stage and try out their material in front of a live audience.
- Acting in school plays and local productions is a good way to get experience.
- Learn by watching. Go to a comedy club or coffeehouse to observe comedians. Watch comedy performances on television or watch videos that feature live stand-up comedians.
- Talk to a comedian about his or her career.

often speak of "paying their dues," which means working in not-so-desirable clubs for critical audiences and for low pay.

It should go without saying that comedians must have a good sense of humor. But being funny is a skill, just like any other. Additionally, some people are simply funnier than others. Many comedians have made jokes or performed humorous skits since they were kids. Comedians need good timing. This means that they can deliver a punch line at just the right moment that makes the audience explode in laughter. If their timing is off, the audience may miss the joke or not react as

Comedians must have excellent stage presence and comedic timing in order to entertain audiences. (Phil McCarten, PictureGroup/AP Photo)

positively. Comedians must also have thick skins because some audiences won't think they are funny. Other important traits for comedians include good storytelling skills, a willingness to travel, and a strong determination to break into the field.

Education and Training

There is no way to become a comedian except to step on a stage and perform. It takes a great deal of work and practice to become a good comedian. It takes many hours on stage to know how to deliver a joke, plan the pace of a show, and figure out on the spot what will make a particular audience laugh.

There are no specific education requirements for comedians, but certain classes can be helpful. English and composition

Words to Learn

closer the last joke a comedian tells before leaving the stage

gig a performance

headliner the main act at a comedy show

impression a comedic imitation of another person that aims to make the audience laugh

improvisation coming up with comedic material quickly without any prior planning or practice

joke a humorous story, impression, improvisation, observation, or sketch that makes people laugh

one-liner a joke that is told in one or two sentences

open mike (or open mic) an event at a comedy club where anybody can get up on stage and perform

punch line the ending of a joke that is supposed to make people laugh

routine a regular collection of jokes told by a comedian to an audience

screenplay the written plan for a movie

sketch a group of short, comedic scenes

Jokes on the Web

These Web sites have lots of jokes to get you started. Practice telling them to friends and classmates. Which jokes get the most laughs?

- 101Kidz: Jokes
  http://www.101kidz.com/jokes

- Ducksters: Jokes
  http://www.ducksters.com/jokesforkids

- Scatty.com
  http://www.scatty.com

- Yahoo! Kids: Jokes
  http://kids.yahoo.com/jokes

will help you write jokes well. Speech and drama classes will help develop your performing skills.

Earnings

Stand-up comedians do not earn regular salaries. They are paid either per show or for a week of performances. Comedians who are starting out may earn as little as $20 for a 20-minute show. Those who perform at colleges earn $250 to $500 per show. Comedians who open a show for the main attraction can earn from $150 to $1,000 per week.

A headline comedian in a comedy club in a large city can earn from $1,000 to $20,000 or more. In smaller clubs, headline comedians make between $300 to $1,000 per show. Those who are just starting out earn very little but can make valuable contacts with club owners, agents, and other comedians. The comedy club usually pays for the comedian's lodging.

FOR MORE INFO

For information on union membership, contact
American Guild of Variety Artists
363 Seventh Avenue, 17th Floor
New York, NY 10001-3904
212-675-1003
agva@agvausa.com
http://www.agvausa.com

Those who write jokes for famous comedians usually get paid around $50 to $100 for every joke used. The writers for a network comedy show can earn anywhere from $50,000 to $150,000 or more a year.

Outlook

There are hundreds of comedy clubs across the country (usually in larger cities). Each club needs performers to get their audiences laughing. The spread of legalized gambling across the United States and the opening of many resorts and theme parks continue to create new opportunities for comedians. There will also be jobs for comedians on television shows and in movies. Comedians will continue to find work into the next decade, but it will be hard to land steady, good-paying work.

Composers

What Composers Do

Who writes the exciting music you hear during movies, television shows, and plays? *Composers* do, that's who. Composers write music for musical stage shows, television commercials, computer and video games, movies, ballet and opera companies, orchestras, pop and rock bands, jazz combos, and other musical performing groups.

Composers work in many different ways. Often they begin with a musical idea and write it down using standard music notation on paper or using a computer software program. They use their music training and their own personal sense of melody, harmony, rhythm, and structure. Some compose music as they play an instrument and may or may not write it down.

Most composers specialize in one style of music, such as classical, jazz, country, rock, or blues. Some combine several styles. Composers who work on commission (payment for a single work or a series of works) or on assign-

EXPLORING

- Read books about composers and composing. See the Browse and Learn More section for some suggestions.
- Participate in musical programs offered by local schools, YMCA/YWCAs, and community centers.
- Learn to play a musical instrument, such as the piano, guitar, violin, or cello.
- Watch movies and television shows and listen to their musical scores.
- Attend concerts and recitals.
- Form or join a musical group and try to write music for your group to perform.
- Talk to a composer about his or her career.

DID YOU KNOW?

Where Composers Work

Most composers are self-employed. They are hired by the following employers to create musical compositions:

- Advertising agencies
- Colleges and universities
- Dance companies
- Film and television production companies
- Musical artists
- Musical theater producers
- Music publishers
- Record companies

ment meet with their clients to discuss the composition's theme, length, style, and the number and types of performers. Composers work at home, in offices, or in music studios. Some need to work alone to plan and build their musical ideas and others work with fellow musicians. Composing can take many long hours of work, and composing jobs may be irregular and low paying. However, composers take great pride in hearing their music performed, and successful commercial music composers can earn a lot of money. After the piece is completed, the composer usually attends rehearsals (practices) and works with the performers. The composer may have to revise parts of the piece until the client is satisfied.

Many composers never perform their own works, but others, especially pop, rock, jazz, country, or blues performers, compose music for their own bands to play.

Education and Training

Take as many music classes as possible—especially those that teach music composition. Participation in school choirs and music groups are also good ways to gain experience in the field.

All composers need to have a good ear and be able to notate, or write down, their music. Composers of musicals, symphonies, and other large works must have years of study in a college, conservatory, or other school of music. Composers of popular songs may not need as much training. However, studying music helps you develop and express your musical ideas better. Music school courses for those who wish to be composers include music theory, musical form, music history, composition, conducting, and arranging. Composers also play at least one musical instrument, usually piano, and some play several instruments.

Earnings

Salaries for all composers ranged from less than $22,000 to $85,000 or more in 2010, according to the U.S. Department of Labor. For music written for the theater, pay is based on the size and type of the theater company or play. Composers for the theater earn from $3,000 to $12,000 per show. A small opera company may pay in the range of $10,000 to $70,000. Large opera companies pay from $15,000 to $150,000. A major film studio may pay a composer $50,000 to $200,000 or more for

Profile: Wolfgang Amadeus Mozart (1756–1791)

Mozart was one of the outstanding masters of the Classical Period (1750–1820 A.D.). He composed works in almost every form. His most famous and respected works are standard repertoire (commonly performed) for piano, symphony orchestra, and opera.

Mozart began his musical studies with his father, Leopold, when he was four years old. He played the clavichord (a stringed keyboard instrument) and harpsichord (a keyboard instrument), and composed minuets (slow, formal dances) and other pieces. At the age of six, with his sister Marianne, Mozart gave concerts in Munich, Germany, and Vienna, Austria. He wrote his first opera, *La finta semplice*, in 1768. At the age of 13, he became director of concerts for the archbishop of Salzburg, Austria.

Mozart died at the age of 35 from illness and overwork. He was buried in an unmarked grave. During his short lifetime, he composed more than 600 works, including more than 25 piano concertos, more than 40 symphonies, and numerous string quartets, piano sonatas, operas, divertimenti, serenades, and dance music.

FOR MORE INFO

For profiles of composers of concert music, visit the ACA Web site.
American Composers Alliance (ACA)
802 West 190th Street, 1st Floor
New York, NY 10040-3937
212-925-0458
info@composers.com
http://composers.com

For educational resources, contact
American Composers Forum
332 Minnesota Street, Suite East 145
St. Paul, MN 55101-1300
651-228-1407
http://www.composersforum.org

For career information, contact
American Federation of Musicians of the United States and Canada
1501 Broadway, Suite 600
New York, NY 10036-5505
212-869-1330
http://www.afm.org

For articles on songwriting and practical information about the business of music, contact
American Society of Composers, Authors, and Publishers
One Lincoln Plaza
New York, NY 10023-7129
212-621-6000
http://www.ascap.com

The IAWM Web site has information for and about women composers.
International Alliance for Women in Music (IAWM)
http://www.iawm.org

The Meet the Composer Web site has information on awards and residencies as well as interviews with composers active in the field today.
Meet the Composer
90 John Street, Suite 312
New York, NY 10038-3243
212-645-6949
mtc@meetthecomposer.org
http://www.meetthecomposer.org

To learn about the annual Young Composer' Competition (for those ages 18 to 30) and other contests, contact
National Association of Composers, USA
PO Box 49256, Barrington Station
Los Angeles, CA 90049-0256
818-274-6048
nacusa@music-usa.org
http://www.music-usa.org/nacusa

For industry information, contact
Society of Composers
PO Box 687
Mineral Wells, TX 76068-0687
http://www.societyofcomposers.org

The society represents composers, lyricists, and songwriters who work in film, television, and multimedia. Visit its Web site for career resources, an online hall of fame, and information on *The SCORE*, its quarterly publication.
Society of Composers & Lyricists
8447 Wilshire Boulevard, Suite 401
Beverly Hills CA 90211-3209
310-281-2812
http://www.thescl.com

a musical score. A composer may be paid per episode for a television program or series, ranging from $1,000 to $10,000 or more.

Outlook

Strong job competition is expected for composers since many people want to enter the field. Despite this prediction, there will continue to be opportunities for composers. As long as there are movies, commercials, television shows, musicals, operas, and other musical performances, there will be a need for composers to write music.

Dancers

What Dancers Do

Dancers use body movements to tell a story, express an idea or feeling, or entertain their audiences. Professional dancers often belong to a dance company, a group of dancers that work together on a repertoire. A repertoire is a collection of dances they perform regularly.

Most dancers study some ballet or classical dance. Classical dance training gives dancers a good foundation for most other types of dance. Many of the standard dance terms used in all types of dance are the same terms used in 17th-century ballet. Traditionally, ballet dance told stories, although today's ballets express a variety of themes and ideas.

Modern dance developed early in the 20th century as a departure from classical ballet. Early modern dancers danced barefoot and began to explore movement and physical expression in new ways. Jazz dance is a form of modern dance often seen in Broadway productions. (Broadway is the nickname for the main theater district in New York City. Many dancers perform there.) Tap dance combines sound and movement as dancers tap out rhythms with metal cleats attached to the toes and heels of their shoes. Other dance forms include ballroom dance, folk or ethnic dance, and acrobatic dance.

Dancers may perform in classical ballets, musical stage shows, folk dance shows, television shows, films, and music videos. Because dancing jobs are not always available, many dancers work as part-time dance instructors. Dancers who create new ballets or dance routines are called *choreographers*.

EXPLORING

- Read books about dance. See the Browse and Learn More section for some suggestions.
- Take as many dance classes as you can. Try different types of dance.
- There are many instructional videos available that teach you ballet, tap, and ballroom dancing. It is best, though, to study with a teacher who can watch you and help you do the movements correctly, so you don't develop bad habits or injure yourself.
- Once you have learned some dance technique, begin to give recitals and performances.
- Audition for school or community stage productions that have dance numbers.
- Watch as many famous dance-oriented movies (*Singin' in the Rain, 42nd Street, A Chorus Line, Staying Alive, Footloose, Chicago,* or *Billy Elliot*) as you can. Note what you like and dislike about the styles of dance and choreography.
- Talk to a dancer about his or her career.
- Visit http://www.ket.org/artstoolkit/dance/glossary.htm for a glossary of dance-related terms.

Dancers begin training early and have fairly short careers. Most professional ballet and modern dancers retire by age 40 because of the physical demands on their bodies. They become dance teachers, artistic directors, choreographers, or they start other careers.

Education and Training

Dancers usually begin training around the age of 10. Some even begin as early as age seven or eight. They may study with

Tap dance legend Savion Glover performs a dance routine. (Kathy Willens, AP Photo)

private teachers or in ballet schools. Dancers who show promise in their early teens may receive professional training in a regional ballet school or a major ballet company. By the age of 17 or 18, dancers begin to audition for positions in professional dance companies.

Many colleges and universities offer degrees in dance with choreography classes. Although you do not need a college degree to become a dancer or choreographer, it can be helpful. Those who teach dance in a college or university often are required to have a degree. Also, since the professional life of a dancer can be rather short, a college degree can give a dancer better options for a second career after retiring from dance performance.

Earnings

The U.S. Department of Labor reports that the median annual salary for full-time dancers was $27,372 in 2010. Salaries ranged from less than $17,000 to $63,000 or more.

Many dancers work part time. Most dance contracts last from 36 to 45 weeks. Modern dance companies usually pay a base salary of $500 to $1,500 per week for a 42- to 44-week season. In smaller companies, pay is about $50 to $100 per performance. Dancers on tour are paid extra for room and board expenses. Minimum performance rates for dancers on television averaged $809 per day in 2010, according to the Screen Actors Guild.

Outlook

Job opportunities for dancers will be fair during the next decade. There will still be more dancers seeking jobs than there are openings. Local ballet companies will offer the most job opportunities. New opportunities are becoming available to dance teachers to help train the public to stay fit using dance techniques.

Tips for Success

To be a successful dancer, you should

- have a love of dancing
- have a lot of drive and ambition
- be a good learner
- be in excellent physical shape
- be agile and graceful
- be willing to work very hard to break into the field

DID YOU KNOW?

Where Dancers Work

- Dance companies
- Local park districts
- Opera companies
- Schools
- Self-employment
- Senior citizens homes
- Social service agencies
- Television production companies
- Theater companies
- Video companies
- Youth centers

FOR MORE INFO

For information on all aspects of dance, contact
American Dance Guild
240 West 14th Street
New York, NY 10011-7218
http://americandanceguild.org

For articles and press releases about dance-related topics, visit the Dance/USA Web site.
Dance/USA
1111 16th Street, NW, Suite 300
Washington, DC 20036-4830
202-833-1717
http://www.danceusa.org

For information on educational programs and a helpful FAQ section, visit

National Association of Schools of Dance (NASD)
11250 Roger Bacon Drive, Suite 21
Reston, VA 20190-5248
703-437-0700
info@arts-accredit.org
http://nasd.arts-accredit.org/index.jsp

For information on careers in dance, contact
National Dance Association
American Alliance for Health, Physical Education, Recreation & Dance
1900 Association Drive
Reston, VA 20191-1598
800-213-7193, ext. 464
http://www.aahperd.org/nda

Disc Jockeys

What Disc Jockeys Do

Disc jockeys, or *DJs*, play recorded music on the radio and the Internet or during parties, dances, and special occasions. On the radio (and sometimes the Internet) they also announce the time, the weather forecast, and important news. Sometimes DJs interview guests, take phone calls from listeners, and make public service announcements.

Unlike radio and television newscasters, disc jockeys most often do not have to read from a written script, except for scripted commercials. Their comments are usually spontaneous (unplanned). Most radio shows are broadcast live, and since anything may happen while DJs are on the air, they must react calmly under stress and know how to handle unexpected events. The best disc jockeys have pleasant, soothing voices and a talent for keeping listeners entertained.

EXPLORING

- Participate in debate or speech clubs to work on your speaking skills and your ability to think and react quickly.
- Try to get a summer job at a radio or Internet station.
- Take advantage of any opportunity to speak or perform before an audience. Try any type of announcing, such as at sports events, awards dinners, or school dances.
- Offer to be the DJ at friends' parties or school dances.
- Record yourself introducing your favorite songs, reading a short news report, or giving weather or traffic information.
- Ask a teacher or counselor to arrange a tour of a local radio station.
- Talk to a disc jockey about his or her career.

Disc jockeys often work irregular hours, and most work alone. Some have to report for work very early in the morning or late at night, because so many radio stations broadcast 24 hours a day. Working at a radio station is demanding. Every activity or comment on the air must begin and end exactly on time. This can be difficult, especially when the disc jockey has to handle news, commercials, music, weather, and guests within a certain time frame. It takes a lot of skill to work the controls, watch the clock, select music, talk with guests or listeners, read reports, and entertain the audience. Usually several of these tasks must be performed at the same time.

Disc jockeys share a laugh during a broadcast. (David Lassman, *Syracuse Newspapers*/The Image Works)

Disc jockeys must always be aware of pleasing their audiences. They play the music their listeners like and talk about the things their listeners want to talk about. If listeners begin to switch stations, ratings go down, and disc jockeys can lose their jobs. Ratings are taken by an outside organization to gauge how many people listen to the station or a particular show. DJs who become popular with their audiences and stay with a station for a long time sometimes become famous in their communities.

Education and Training

In high school, take English classes and speech classes to help you develop your communication skills. Extracurricular activities such as debate clubs and theater will also help you learn good pronunciation and how to project your voice. Music classes will introduce you to musical styles, techniques, and artists. If your high school has a radio station, be sure to volunteer as a disc jockey, producer, or technician.

There is no formal education required for disc jockeys. Many large radio stations prefer to hire people who have had some college education. Some schools train students for broadcasting, but such training will not necessarily improve the chances of finding a job at a radio station. When hiring DJs, station managers consider an applicant's personality and listen carefully to his or her audition recordings.

DID YOU KNOW?

- There were 14,355 radio stations in the United States as of June 2009.
- The average American listens to radio two hours and 14 minutes a day.
- The top three radio formats in fall 2008 were news/talk/information, country, and adult contemporary.

Sources: Federal Communications Commission, Radio Advertising Bureau, Arbitron

DID YOU KNOW?

The first major contemporary disc jockey in the United States was Alan Freed (1921–1965), who worked in the 1950s on WINS radio in New York. In 1957, his rock and roll stage shows at the Paramount Theater made front-page news in the *New York Times* because of the huge crowds they attracted. The title "disc jockey" started because most music was recorded on conventional flat records or discs.

FOR MORE INFO

For information about broadcast education and the broadcasting industry, contact
Broadcast Education Association
1771 N Street, NW
Washington, DC 20036-2891
202-429-3935
http://www.beaweb.org

To read answers to frequently asked questions about broadcasting, visit the NAB Web site.
National Association of Broadcasters (NAB)
1771 N Street, NW
Washington, DC 20036-2800

202-429-5300
nab@nab.org
http://www.nab.org

Visit the association's Web site to read career articles.
Radio Television Digital News Association
529 14th Street, NW, Suite 425
Washington, DC 20045-1406
202-659-6510
http://www.rtdna.org

If you want to become a disc jockey and possibly advance to other broadcasting positions, attend a college or technical school that has broadcasting or announcing programs. Working at a college radio station can give you valuable experience. Many DJs start out at small radio stations operating equipment and recording interviews.

Earnings

Disc jockeys earned salaries that ranged from less than $17,000 to more than $72,000 annually in 2010, according to the U.S. Department of Labor. The mean annual salary was $38,610 a year. Those who work for small stations earn the lowest salaries. Top personalities in large market stations earn salaries that range from $100,000 to more than $1 million annually.

Outlook

In the broadcasting field there are usually more job applicants than job openings. As a result, competition is stiff. Beginning jobs in small radio stations usually are easiest to find. Employment of disc jockeys is expected to decline over the next several years. Due to this decline, competition will be fierce in an already competitive field.

Small stations will still hire beginners, but on-air experience will be increasingly important. You may have an advantage over other job applicants if you know a lot about a specific area such as business, political, or health news, or if you have an extensive knowledge of a particular kind of music, such as jazz, rock, rap, or country.

Satellite and Internet radio should provide some new job opportunities, but many jobs in these new fields are part time and low paying.

Film and Television Directors

What Film and Television Directors Do

Film and television directors coordinate the making of a movie or television show. Others direct television news broadcasts, game and talk shows, sporting events, and other types of productions.

Directors are involved in every stage of creating a movie, television show, or other feature—from hiring actors to helping edit the final product. Film directors are also called *filmmakers* and *motion picture directors.*

While *producers* are in charge of the business and financial side of a project, directors are in charge of the creative and technical sides. Usually a producer hires the director, but they work closely together. They plan a budget and production schedule, including time for research, casting (choosing actors), set design, filming, and editing.

Directors give directions before, during, and after production to many different people. They choose costumes, scenery, and music. During rehearsals, they plan the action carefully, telling actors how to move and interpret the script. They coach the actors to help them give their best performances. At the same time, directors give directions for sets and lighting, and decide on the order and angles of camera shots. Once filming is finished, they supervise editing and provide suggestions on sound and special effects.

Film directors work on feature films, documentaries, made-for-TV movies, industrial films, and travelogues. *Directors of computer-generated animation* manage animators and artists who create animated movies and television shows. They check

EXPLORING

- Read books about a career as a director. See the Browse and Learn More section for some suggestions.
- Watch movies and television shows every chance you get, both at the theater and at home. Notice what makes them interesting, from camera angles to soundtrack choices.
- Many DVDs offer special features where directors talk about the making of the film or television show. Listen to these features to learn more about what it takes to be successful in the field.
- Two major trade publications to read are *Variety* (http://www.variety.com) and *Hollywood Reporter* (http://www.hollywoodreporter.com).
- Talk to a director about his or her career.

that their work meets design standards and that the story is being told in an effective way. They also work with production designers, art directors, and other production staff to make sure the project is manageable and meeting scheduling demands. Some television directors work on regular shows or series, such as soap operas, situation comedies, sporting events, talk shows, and game shows. These directors work at a console with a row of television monitors. The monitors show what is going on in different parts of the studio from different camera angles.

Most directors work on a freelance basis. They are hired by film studios (both major and independent), television stations, and cable networks. They also might develop their own independent projects. Some directors teach at colleges and universities.

A director outlines an upcoming scene for an actress and a production crew.
(Warner Brothers Pictures/Topham/The Image Works)

Education and Training

You can start now to prepare for a career in directing. Take English literature classes to learn storytelling techniques. Theater classes will teach you about acting. Photography courses can teach you about visual composition. Your school may even offer film or video production classes. If so, take as many of these courses as possible.

Even though there are no specific requirements for becoming a director, the most successful directors have a wide variety of talents and experience, as well as good business and management skills. You must be able to develop ideas, and be good at communicating with others.

Today, many directors have degrees in film or television direction, film studies, cinematography, or related fields. There are many colleges and universities that offer film or media majors with a concentration in directing. These programs require you to direct your own films. They also offer internship and other practical learning experiences. The Directors Guild of America offers an Assistant Directors Training Program for those who have a bachelor's degree or two years of experience in movie production. (See For More Info).

Profile: Kathryn Bigelow (1951–   )

In 2010, Kathryn Bigelow made movie history when she won the Academy Award for Best Director for her picture, *The Hurt Locker.* She was the first woman ever to receive this award.

Born in San Carlos, California, Bigelow originally hoped to be an artist. She studied at the San Francisco Art Institute, and later at the prestigious Whitney Museum of American Arts Independent Study program.

Bigelow began her film career soon after graduation from Columbia University's film program. Her first movie, *The Set-Up,* was a 20-minute film that analyzed the use of violence in movies. Bigelow's other notable films include *Near Dark* (1987), *Blue Steel* (1989), *Point Break* (1991), *Strange Days* (1995), *The Weight of Water* (2000), and *K-19: The Widowmaker* (2002).

The Hurt Locker, Bigelow's best-known picture to date, follows her penchant for making gritty, male-oriented action movies that touch on issues of violence and tension. This movie tells the story of bomb detonation experts during the Iraq War.

Bigelow was also awarded the Best Director awards from the Directors Guild of America, the British Academy of Film and Television Arts, and other organizations for her work on *The Hurt Locker.* The movie also garnered Bigelow a second Oscar, for her work as producer.

Sources: *Time, Newsweek*

Tips for Success

To be a successful film and television director, you should

- be very creative
- be able to handle stress and meet deadlines
- have leadership skills
- be organized
- have good communication skills
- be willing to work long hours to meet production deadlines

Earnings

Salaries for directors ranged from less than $33,000 to more than $166,000 in 2010, according to the U.S. Department of Labor. The mean annual salary of film directors was $109,860. Television directors earned $72,030. Top movie directors can earn millions of dollars per project.

Outlook

The number of movies and television shows being made is increasing as the cable television and video-rental industries continue to expand. Demand is also growing for directors to create movies and other content for viewing on portable electronic devices and on the Internet. Despite increasing interest in television shows, movies, and sporting events, many people are interested in becoming directors and there will be stiff competition for jobs. Directors with strong artistic ability and college training will have the best job prospects.

FOR MORE INFO

For a variety of movie-related resources, visit the AFI Web site.

American Film Institute (AFI)
2021 North Western Avenue
Los Angeles, CA 90027-1657
323-856-7600
information@afi.com
http://www.afi.com

For information about broadcast education and the broadcasting industry, contact

Broadcast Education Association
1771 N Street, NW
Washington, DC 20036-2891
202-429-3935
http://www.beaweb.org

For information on a career as a director, contact

Directors Guild of America
7920 Sunset Boulevard
Los Angeles, CA 90046-3300

310-289-2000
http://www.dga.org

For information on movie ratings, contact

Motion Picture Association of America
1600 Eye Street, NW
Washington, DC 20006-4010
202-293-1966
http://www.mpaa.org

Women in Film's mission is to "empower, promote, and mentor women in the entertainment and media industries." Visit its Web site for more information.

Women in Film
6100 Wilshire Boulevard, Suite 710
Los Angeles, CA 90048-5107
323-935-2211
info@wif.org
http://www.wif.org

Magicians

What Magicians Do

Magicians are masters of illusion. They use a combination of complicated moves and convincing comments to make audiences believe they can pull a rabbit out of a hat, make objects appear and disappear, and make people float in mid-air.

Magicians use tricks and a variety of props, such as illusion boxes, cards, or coins. They often use volunteers from the audience. For example, they might secretly remove a volunteer's watch and make it reappear in someone else's pocket. Or, a magician may use a wooden box or other prop to appear to cut a trained assistant in half with a saw. Each magician has a unique style and many specialize in one type of magic, such as card tricks, or escape art (getting out of locked boxes, chains, etc.).

There are two basic elements to a magician's performance. The first element is the technique, the actual mechanics of performing illusions or tricks. Magicians practice each movement many times until they can do the trick perfectly.

EXPLORING

- You can begin to learn magic tricks on your own by reading books about the field. See the Browse and Learn More section for some suggestions.
- Visit a magic shop to explore the different kinds of props and tools magicians use. Magic shops may also have bulletin boards with postings of club meetings or workshops in your area.
- Once you learn a few tricks, begin to perform for your family and friends.
- Talk to a magician about his or her career.

A magician performs his act. (Damian Dovarganes, AP Photo)

The magician's presentation of an illusion is the second element. The illusions must be exciting and entertaining to keep the audience's attention. Magicians are masters at directing an audience's attention to certain areas and away from others with flashy movements and verbal distractions.

Magicians usually work indoors in front of audiences. They may perform in front of large crowds at a theater or for just a few people at a birthday party. They often work alone, but they sometimes use one or two assistants.

Most magicians are self-employed. They are hired for everything from private parties to major stage shows in Las Vegas or on Broadway (the main theater district in New York City).

Education and Training

Magicians are skilled entertainers. It can take years of practice to become an accomplished magician, but it is often possible to learn some basic tricks in just a short time.

Professional magicians rarely tell how they perform their tricks. Because of this code of silence, the most common form of training is for a budding magician to study with a professional magician. Many beginning magicians start their careers as assistants for more experienced magicians.

People generally do not take college or high school courses to learn magic tricks, although courses in acting or public speaking can improve your performance skills. You also need to learn good business skills, as magicians usually must handle their own financial matters.

Earnings

While world-famous magicians, such as David Copperfield, can earn many thousands of dollars for each performance, most magicians do not earn enough from their performances to support themselves financially. They often perform nights or on weekends and have other full- or part-time jobs. A magician may earn anywhere from $50 for performing at a birth-

Tips for Success

To be a successful magician, you should

- have excellent hand-eye coordination
- have good agility to quickly move wooden boxes, tables, or other props
- be able to learn new tricks
- be able to use your imagination to make old tricks seem fresh
- have an excellent stage presence
- be comfortable performing in front of various groups of people
- be willing to travel frequently for work

Famous Magicians

Performers such as the Sicilian Count Alessandro di Cagliostro (1743–1795), the Frenchman Jean Eugène Robert-Houdin (1805–1871), and the American Harry Houdini (1874–1926), captured the imaginations of audiences with their skill, training, and imagination.

In recent times, magic has lost some of its mystery and become accepted as a performance art. Today, well-known magicians such as David Copperfield and Lance Burton, entertain people all over the world. More controversial are the popular and less-traditional duo Penn & Teller, who sometimes reveal the secrets of their illusions to their audiences.

day party to several thousand dollars for performing at a business meeting or magic show. Many magicians remain amateurs, and some practicing magicians view magic and performing as a hobby, rather than as a career. According to the Society of American Magicians, those who work part time earn as much as $15,000 to $20,000 a year, while full-time professionals may earn as much as $60,000 to $120,000 a year.

Average annual salaries for full-time entertainers and performers, not otherwise classified (a category that includes magicians) were $29,827 in 2010, according to the U.S. Department of Labor. Salaries ranged from less than $19,000 to $69,000 or more. Entertainers and performers who worked at amusement parks earned mean annual salaries of $28,974.

Outlook

It is tough to have a successful career as a magician. Highly skilled magicians should find job opportunities, while those just

FOR MORE INFO

For information on conventions, publications, and local groups (called "Rings") that provide lectures and demonstrations, contact
International Brotherhood of Magicians
13 Point West Boulevard
St. Charles, MO 63301-4431
636-724-2400
http://www.magician.org

For information on local organizations, publications, and youth programs and membership, contact
Society of American Magicians
PO Box 2900
Pahrump, NV 89041-2900
http://www.magicsam.com

starting out in the field may find it difficult to find work. To be successful, magicians must spend a lot of time promoting themselves and hunting for jobs at parties, special events, business meetings, schools, fairs, amusement parks, and conventions.

Music Teachers

What Music Teachers Do

Music teachers teach people how to sing, play musical instruments, and appreciate and enjoy the world of music. They teach private lessons and classes. They may work at home or in a studio, school, college, or conservatory (a special music school). Many music teachers are also performing musicians.

Teachers help students learn to read music, develop their voices, breathe correctly, and hold and play their instruments properly. As their students master the techniques of their art, teachers guide them through more and more difficult pieces of music. Music teachers often organize recitals or concerts that feature their students. These recitals allow family and friends to hear how well the students are progressing and helps students get performing experience.

Private music teachers may teach children who are just beginning to play or sing, teens who hope to make music their career, or adults who are interested in music lessons for their own enjoyment. They teach these students in a studio, at their students' homes, or in their own homes.

EXPLORING

- Sing in your school or church choir. Join a band or orchestra. Get as much experience as you can playing, singing, and performing.
- Read all you can about music theory, music history, famous musicians, and performance.
- Talk to your music teachers about what they like and don't like about teaching music. Ask them how they became music teachers.

Music teachers in elementary and secondary schools often offer group and private lessons. They direct in-school glee clubs, concert choirs, marching bands, or orchestras. College and university teachers are also often performers or composers. They divide their time between group and individual instruction and may teach several music subjects, such as music appreciation, music history, theory (the study of the structure of music), and pedagogy (the teaching of music).

Education and Training

If you are interested in becoming a music teacher, you probably are already taking voice lessons or are learning to play

A music teacher helps a student with a keyboard exercise. (Tina Fineberg, AP Photo)

Learning an Instrument

About.com lists the following instruments as the easiest to learn for beginners:

- Cello
- Clarinet
- Double bass
- Flute
- Guitar
- Harp
- Piano
- Saxophone
- Trumpet
- Violin

an instrument. Participation in music classes, choral groups, bands, and orchestras are also good ways to prepare for a career teaching music.

Like all musicians, music teachers spend years mastering their instruments or developing their voices. Private teachers need no formal training or licenses, but most have spent years studying with an experienced musician, either in a school or conservatory or through private lessons.

Teachers in public elementary schools and high schools must have a state-issued teaching license. Hundreds of conservatories, universities, and colleges offer bachelor's degrees in music education to qualify students for state certificates.

To teach music in colleges and schools of music or in conservatories, you must usually have a graduate degree in music. However, very talented and well-known performers or composers are sometimes hired without any formal graduate training. Only a few people reach that level of fame.

DID YOU KNOW?

Where Music Teachers Work

- Colleges and universities
- Community centers
- Elementary and middle schools
- High schools
- Religious organizations

FOR MORE INFO

To read about the issues affecting teachers, contact the following organizations:

American Association of University Professors
1133 19th Street, NW, Suite 200
Washington, DC 20036-3655
202-737-5900
http://www.aaup.org

American Federation of Teachers
555 New Jersey Avenue, NW
Washington, DC 20001-2079
202-879-4400
http://www.aft.org

National Education Association
1201 16th Street, NW
Washington, DC 20036-3290
202-833-4000
http://www.nea.org

For a directory of U.S. and Canadian music programs and statistics on music education, visit the CMS Web site.
The College Music Society (CMS)
312 East Pine Street
Missoula, MT 59802-4624
406-721-9616
cms@music.org
http://www.music.org

To participate in online forums about music education and to read a variety of useful online brochures, such as *Careers in Music* and *How to Nail a College Entrance Audition*, visit the following Web site:

MENC: The National Association for Music Education
1806 Robert Fulton Drive
Reston, VA 20191-4341
800-336-3768
http://www.menc.org

For information on music education, contact
Music Teachers National Association
441 Vine Street, Suite 3100
Cincinnati, OH 45202-3004
888-512-5278
mtnanet@mtna.org
http://www.mtna.org

For information on choosing a music school and a database of accredited music schools in the United States, visit the NASM Web site.
National Association of Schools of Music (NASM)
11250 Roger Bacon Drive, Suite 21
Reston, VA 20190-5248
703-437-0700
info@arts-accredit.org
http://nasm.arts-accredit.org

For information on teacher accreditation, contact
National Council for Accreditation of Teacher Education
2010 Massachusetts Avenue, NW, Suite 500
Washington, DC 20036-1023
202-466-7496
ncate@ncate.org
http://www.ncate.org

Earnings

Salaries for music teachers vary depending on the type of teaching, the number of hours spent teaching, and the skill of the teacher. According to MENC: The National Association for Music Education, early childhood music educators earn $6 to $60/hour, while studio music teachers earn $10 to $100/hour. Full-time music teachers at the elementary and secondary levels earn salaries that range from $35,000 to $83,000 annually. The U.S. Department of Labor reports that college music teachers earned median annual salaries of $62,040 in 2010.

Outlook

Opportunities for music teachers are expected to grow at an average rate in elementary schools and colleges and universities, but at a slower rate in secondary schools. When schools face budget problems, music and other art programs are often the first to be cut. Competition has also increased as more instrumental musicians enter teaching because of the lack of performing jobs.

Musical Instrument Repairers

EXPLORING

- Read books about musical instruments. See the Browse and Learn More section for some suggestions.
- Take music lessons or classes to develop your musical "ear."
- Learn to play a variety of instruments.
- Study physics to learn about the mechanics of sound.
- Shop classes and art classes can teach you woodworking and metalworking skills.
- Hobbies, such as jewelry making and model building, help you learn to handle fine tools and small parts.
- Talk to a musical instrument repairer about his or her career.

What Musical Instrument Repairers Do

Musical instrument repairers tune instruments and make other repairs as needed. Most repairers specialize in fixing one type of instrument—such as pianos, guitars, or brass instruments. Many repairers make regular inspections of pianos, organs, or other instruments to keep them from getting out of tune or developing other problems.

When a piano or other large instrument gets out of tune or develops other problems, repairers make house calls. Piano repairs, for example, range from adjusting a string to the proper pitch to replacing the wooden sounding board that amplifies the sound of the strings. Repairers use screwdrivers, pliers, and other hand tools as well as special restringing tools.

Musical instrument repairers who work on guitars, violins, and other small string instruments play the instrument to listen for particular problems and adjust strings or make other repairs. Repairers may have to take the instrument apart to find a problem or make a repair. They use hand tools, such as screwdrivers and pliers, to remove cracked or broken sections. They often use a variety of glues and varnishes.

Wind-instrument repairers work on clarinets, oboes, bassoons, saxophones, and flutes. Common repairs include fixing or replacing the moving parts of the instrument, cutting new padding or corks to replace worn pieces, and replacing springs. If the body of the woodwind is cracked in any sections the repairer tries to pin or glue the crack shut. In some situations, the repairer must replace the entire section or joint of the instrument.

Repairing brass instruments such as trumpets and French horns requires skill in metal working and plating. To fix dents, the repairer works the dent out with hammers and more delicate tools and seals splits in the metal with solder (a type of metal that is heated). If one of the valves of the brass instrument is leaking, the repairer may replate it and build up layers of metal to fill the gaps.

Percussion tuners and *repairers* work on drums, bells, congas, timbales, cymbals, and castanets. They may stretch new skins over the instrument, replace broken or missing parts, or seal cracks in the wood.

Education and Training

Musical instrument repairers do not have to be expert musicians, but they should be able to play an instrument and know when it is out of tune. Repairers must be able to talk to customers and be able to explain what is wrong with an instrument. Speech and English classes will help you develop your communication skills. Other important classes include physics, art, and shop.

Most repairers learn their skills through an apprenticeship. They work in music shops under the supervision of experienced repairers. It takes four to five years of training to become a skilled piano or organ repairer. It takes less time to become qualified

DID YOU KNOW?

Scientists have uncovered what might be the oldest playable musical instrument, reports the scientific journal *Nature.* They found six complete bone flutes between 7,000 and 9,000 years old at the early Neolithic site of Jiahu in China.

The flutes are all made from the ulnae, or wing bones, of the red-crowned crane and have five, six, seven, or eight holes. You can hear an audio recording of the flute and read more about the discovery at http://www.bnl.gov/bnlweb/flutes.html.

Tests at the Music School of the Art Institute of China showed that the flute's seven holes produce a tone scale similar to the Western eight-note scale that begins "do, re, mi."

The oldest known musical instruments were recently found in the Hohle Fels cavern in southwest Germany. They are 35,000 years old and made of bird bones and mammoth tusks. The original instruments cannot be played, but scientists have built replicas that allow them to hear their ancient sounds.

in fixing smaller musical instruments. It can take many years to learn how to repair violins and other fine-stringed instruments.

A few technical schools offer programs in instrument repair. These programs last from six months to two years. Although they offer some hands-on experience, you would be wise to get additional training with an experienced musical instrument repairer before you start out on your own.

Earnings

Musical instrument repairers and tuners earned salaries that ranged from less than $19,000 to more than $56,000 a year in 2010, according to the U.S. Department of Labor. The average salary was $31,760. Earnings are usually higher in urban areas.

Outlook

Although there are millions of instruments in the United States, relatively few people make a living as musical instrument repairers. This situation is not expected to change over the next decade. Most instrument repairers are self-employed and may not have the time to train new workers. Those with the most training will have the best chance at job opportunities. More repairers and tuners will be needed to work on instruments rented to students, schools, and other organizations. Since music programs are being cut at schools, there will be less need for repairers.

Tips for Success

To be a successful musical instrument repairer, you should

- have an interest in music
- have good hearing and eyesight
- be good with your hands
- have excellent communication skills
- be willing to continue to learn throughout your career
- have discipline in order to stay with a project until it is finished
- have good business skills if you own your own business

FOR MORE INFO

The GAL is an international organization of stringed-instrument makers and repairers. Visit its Web site for information on building and repairing instruments.
Guild of American Luthiers (GAL)
http://www.luth.org

For information about band instrument repair and a list of schools offering courses and degrees in the field, contact
National Association of Professional Band Instrument Repair Technicians
PO Box 51
2026 Eagle Road
Normal, IL 61761-0051
309-452-4257
http://www.napbirt.org

For information on certification and training programs, contact
Piano Technicians Guild
4444 Forest Avenue
Kansas City, KS 66106-3750
913-432-9975
ptg@ptg.org
http://www.ptg.org

What Musicians Do

Musicians perform, teach, write, arrange, and direct music. *Instrumental musicians* play one or more musical instruments, usually in a group. They play in jazz bands, country and western bands, symphony orchestras, dance bands, pop or rock bands, or other groups. The human voice is also a musical instrument. *Singers*, or *vocalists*, are those who create music with their voices.

Classical musicians perform in orchestra concerts, opera and dance performances, and theater orchestras. The most talented may work as soloists with orchestras. Some accompany singers, choirs, and solo musicians on the piano during rehearsals and performances. Classical musicians also perform in churches or accompany church choirs.

Musicians in jazz, blues, country, and pop or rock groups play in bars, nightclubs, festivals, and concert halls. They may perform music for recordings, television, videos, and movie soundtracks. Musicians who play popular music almost always use rhythm instruments, such as piano, bass, drums, and guitar in their groups. They also add melody, harmony, and special effects with all kinds of other acoustic and electronic instruments, such as brass, woodwinds, and synthesizers. Some instruments are unique to one type of music. For example, country and western music often features the slide guitar, banjo, and fiddle. Blues musicians often play harmonica. However, talented musicians can play any type of music on their instruments. Some musicians, especially classical

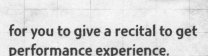

EXPLORING

- Read books about music theory and musical instruments. See the Browse and Learn More section for some suggestions.
- Schools and communities give you lots of choices for musical training and performance, including choirs, ensembles, bands, orchestras, musicals, and talent shows.
- If you are taking private lessons, your teacher can arrange for you to give a recital to get performance experience.
- Religious organizations provide opportunities for singers, instrumentalists, and directors to perform and learn.
- Summer music camps give you a chance to perform with others, gain experience on stage, and begin to find out if you have what it takes to become a professional musician.
- Talk to a musician about his or her career.

musicians, focus on playing one instrument. Others play several instruments, although they often have one instrument that they specialize in.

Many musicians travel a great deal, and few are able to find full-time work. Most have periods of unemployment between jobs and support themselves with other work during the day. Musicians find work all over the country, but most jobs are found in large cities and in areas with large recording industries.

Education and Training

Many colleges and universities have music departments that offer degrees in music, but a music degree is not required for most jobs in instrumental music. Courses in music, math, and social science are helpful. Participation in band or choir is useful preparation for a music career. Community groups also offer training and performance in music, dance, singing, and theater. These activities will give you performance experience.

Instrumental musicians begin developing their musical skills at an early age. From then on, long hours of practice and study are necessary. Most musicians train under the supervision of an experienced musician. In addition to learning the technique for an instrument, such as fingering patterns, breathing, embouchure (mouth position for brass and wind players), and tone, musicians also learn music theory, including rhythm, melody, harmony, and notation.

Earnings

Musicians in the major U.S. symphony orchestras earn average salaries of $70,000, according to MENC: The National Association for Music Education. The median salary for musicians and singers was $46,571 in 2010, according to the U.S. Department of Labor. Popular musicians are paid per gig. Average pay per musician ranges from $30 to $300 per performance. Of course, musicians who are well known earn hundreds of thousands

Profile: John Coltrane (1926–1967)

Jazz musician John Coltrane began his professional career performing in bars and clubs in Philadelphia. He played in the bands of jazz greats such as Dizzy Gillespie, Thelonious Monk, and Miles Davis. Coltrane made his first album in 1957 and formed his own band in 1960. He played both soprano and tenor saxophone and influenced many musicians with his avant-garde (cutting edge), improvisatory style. Visit http://www.johncoltrane.com to learn more about John Coltrane.

Words to Learn

chord a combination of three or more tones at the same time that make up a single block of harmony

counterpoint the use of more than one melody at the same time

harmony a combination of musical notes mixed with intervals and chords

improvisation creating music on the spot, as opposed to performing music that was composed previously

interval in music, the distance between two pitches

key a scale that provides the harmonic material for a piece of music (a piece of music that is based on the C major scale, for example, is said to be "in the key" of C major)

lyrics the words of a song

melody a succession of single pitches or tones

notation a written system representing musical sounds

pitch the lowness or highness of a tone

rhythm the organized movement of a musical composition over time

scale a particular set of notes arranged in an ascending or descending order

tempo Italian for speed; the speed at which a piece of music is played

timbre the particular quality of sound of a voice or instrument

tone a sound of a particular pitch

or even millions of dollars each year, but very few musicians achieve such earnings and fame. Studio recording work pays musicians well but is not plentiful. Church organists, choir directors, and soloists earn about $40 to $100 each week, but these positions often are part time.

Outlook

It is very difficult to earn a living solely as a musician. Competition for jobs will be strong in the next decade. Musicians who can play multiple instruments and are familiar with more than

FOR MORE INFO

For information on education and careers, contact
American Federation of Musicians of the United States and Canada
1501 Broadway, Suite 600
New York, NY 10036-5501
212-869-1330
http://www.afm.org

The AGMA is a union for professional musicians. Visit its Web site for more information about the field.
American Guild of Musical Artists (AGMA)
1430 Broadway, 14th Floor
New York, NY 10018-3308
212-265-3687
http://www.musicalartists.org

To participate in online forums about music education and to read a variety of useful online brochures, such as *Careers in Music* and *How to Nail a College Entrance Audition*, visit the following Web site:
MENC: The National Association for Music Education
1806 Robert Fulton Drive
Reston, VA 20191-4341

800-336-3768
http://www.menc.org

For information on music education, contact
Music Teachers National Association
441 Vine Street, Suite 3100
Cincinnati, OH 45202-3004
888-512-5278
http://www.mtna.org

For information on choosing a music school and a database of accredited music schools in the United States, visit the NASM Web site.
National Association of Schools of Music (NASM)
11250 Roger Bacon Drive, Suite 21
Reston, VA 20190-5248
703-437-0700
info@arts-accredit.org
http://nasm.arts-accredit.org

This organization offers networking opportunities, career information, and a mentoring program for women in music.
Women In Music
http://womeninmusic.org

one musical style (such as jazz, rock, or country music) will have the best job prospects. Religious organizations will provide the most new jobs. Self-employed musicians who play in clubs and other musical settings will not have as good job opportunities.

Orchestra Conductors

What Orchestra Conductors Do

An orchestra is a group of musicians who play music together. *Orchestra conductors* are the men and women who direct the musicians as they play. Usually, the word orchestra applies to groups larger than six musicians. Smaller groups are called trios, combos, quintets, or bands. Orchestras play many different types of music. Some play jazz, others play dance music, and still others play classical music.

Orchestra conductors have many responsibilities. Their most important task is to decide how a piece of music should be played and then to teach the musicians in the orchestra to play the piece that way. In other words, the conductor helps the orchestra to interpret a piece of music.

In addition to interpreting music, conductors help orchestras to play as a unit. A symphony orchestra, for example, may have 50 to 80 musicians who play a variety of instruments. Each

EXPLORING

- Go to as many musical presentations as you can—symphonies, operas, musical theater—and study the conductors. Note their baton techniques and their arm and body movements. Try to determine how the orchestra and audience respond to the gesturing of the conductors.
- Read reference books and biographies about conductors and their work. See the Browse and Learn More section for some suggestions.
- Talk to a conductor about his or her career.

group of instruments, such as violins or French horns, has a slightly different musical line to play. Without a strong conductor it would be difficult for all of these musicians to produce a pleasing sound. The conductor sets the beat, decides when the music should be played louder or softer, and indicates which instruments should play at what times. Most conductors use a baton and arm and body movements to direct the orchestra during a performance. There is no single way to use a baton. Some conductors use only very minimal baton movements. Others use sweeping baton strokes and broad arm and body gestures.

Conductors work with many different types of orchestras. Some conductors lead symphony orchestras. Others direct orchestras that play during operas, musical plays, or ballet performances. Conductors also lead marching bands, jazz bands, and dance bands.

Orchestra conductors are employed by orchestras of all sizes, theaters, opera companies, musical groups associated with broadcasting, and film studios. Some teach at music conservatories and colleges and universities.

Education and Training

Conductors should be able to play one or more instruments and must know music theory, analysis, composition, notation, and sight-reading. They need the skills to control the timing, rhythm, and structure of a musical piece. They must command the attention and respect of orchestra members.

There are no formal education requirements for conductors. However, most study music throughout their whole lives. Some conservatories and universities offer conducting programs. Many of the conductor's skills are learned and developed in practice.

Some schools offer courses in music and music appreciation. Other helpful classes include math, dance, and theater. Many schools have student bands and orchestras. However, serious music students usually attend special music schools, called conservatories. Students also study with private teachers.

Fame & Fortune: Marin Alsop (b. 1956)

Marin Alsop is a groundbreaking female conductor, musical director, and musician. In September 2007, she was appointed the music director of the Baltimore Symphony Orchestra, becoming the first woman to lead a major American orchestra.

Alsop was born on October 16, 1956, in New York City. Her parents were professional musicians. They encouraged her to experiment with musical instruments at a very young age. Alsop had great musical ability. She began taking piano lessons at age two and violin studies at age five! At the age of nine, Alsop heard the world-famous conductor Leonard Bernstein conduct the New York Philharmonic and announced that she wanted to become a conductor.

Alsop excelled at school and in her musical training. In fact, she entered Yale University at the age of 16. She eventually transferred to The Julliard School and received bachelor's and master's degrees in violin performance.

It may seem that everything came easy for Alsop, but this is not true. She had to spend hours practicing the violin and pursuing her studies. While many women are musicians, only a few work as conductors. Through hard work, talent, and determination, Alsop became the first woman to head a major U.S. orchestra. Her achievement has inspired young women from around the world to consider a career in music. In 2002, Alsop founded the Taki Concordia Conducting Fellowship to help young women conductors learn about the "art and business of performing classical music." Her advice to young people: "Pursue that which you are passionate about and pure and simply never give up! If the front door is locked to you, go around the side and sneak in a window!!"

Visit http://www.marinalsop.com to learn more about Marin Alsop's career.

Sources: MarinAlsop.com

DID YOU KNOW?

Many different conducting styles emerged in the 20th century, including some that were quite dramatic. Sir Thomas Beecham (1879–1961), the great British conductor, sometimes raised his arms skyward imploring the orchestra to reach perfection. At other times he lunged at the horn section to raise its power, occasionally falling off the podium in his enthusiasm. Leopold Stokowski (1882–1977) and Leonard Bernstein (1918–1990) were also noted for their dramatic flair.

Earnings

The range of earnings for conductors varies greatly from one category of conductors to another. Many conductors work part time and have small yearly incomes. Part-time choir directors for churches and synagogues earn $3,500 to $25,000 per year, while full-time directors make from $15,000 to $40,000. Dance band conductors earn $300 to $1,200 per week. Opera and choral group conductors make $8,000 a year working part time at the community level. Those with permanent positions with established companies in major cities can earn more than $100,000 a year. Symphony orchestra conductors earn $35,000 to $50,000 a year or more conducting smaller, regional orchestras. The resident conductor of an internationally famous orchestra can earn $500,000 or more a year.

Choir, orchestra, and opera conductors earn salaries that range from $15,000 to $275,000 a year, according to MENC: The National Association for Music Education.

Outlook

It will be hard to land a job as a conductor for a major orchestra. There will be more opportunities with smaller orchestras. Conductors with a lot of musical talent and experience will have the best chances of landing top jobs.

FOR MORE INFO

For information on union membership, contact
American Federation of Musicians of the United States and Canada
1501 Broadway, Suite 600
New York, NY 10036-5501
212-869-1330
http://www.afm.org

For information on union membership, contact
American Guild of Musical Artists
1430 Broadway, 14th Floor
New York, NY 10018-3308
212-265-3687
http://www.musicalartists.org

For conducting resources, contact
Conductors Guild
719 Twinridge Lane
Richmond, VA 23235-5270
804-553-1378
guild@conductorsguild.org
http://www.conductorsguild.org

For information on orchestra careers, contact
League of American Orchestras
33 West 60th Street, 5th Floor
New York, NY 10023-7905
212-262-5161
http://www.americanorchestras.org

This organization represents the professional interests of female band directors. Visit its Web site for information on membership for high school and college students.
Women Band Directors International
http://www.womenbanddirectors.org

For information on auditions and competitions in Canada, contact
Orchestras Canada
203-460 College Street
Toronto, ON M6G 1A1 Canada
416-366-8834
http://www.oc.ca

Pop and Rock Musicians

What Pop and Rock Musicians Do

Pop and rock musicians perform in clubs, concert halls, on college campuses, and at festivals and fairs. They often write original music and perform it with other instrumentalists and vocalists.

After writing the music, musicians spend many hours practicing or rehearsing the new songs with other band members. Rehearsal and commitment to the band is extremely important to rock musicians. In order for the band to sound as good as it possibly can, all the instrumentalists and vocalists must work together and get to know each other's abilities and styles.

Pop and rock musicians record a demo (demonstration) recording, which they send to club managers and music producers. When making a demo, or recording a CD for a record company, they record in a studio and work with recording professionals, such as audio engineers, producers, and mixing engineers. Musicians may also have to audition live for a club manager in addition to providing a demo recording.

When a club books, or hires, a band, the club's promotional staff may advertise the upcoming performance. Many bands, though, have to attract audiences on their own. They distribute fliers, send press releases to area newspapers, and send out announcements. A popular way to promote a band is to have a Web site listing performance schedules, photos and videos of the band members, and a few free songs or entire albums for download. Many musicians now use social media such as MySpace, Facebook, and Twitter to tell their fans about their

EXPLORING

- Become involved in your school's various musical groups.
- Read books about pop and rock music and musicians. See the Browse and Learn More section for some suggestions.
- Read books about music theory and musical instruments. See the Browse and Learn More section for some suggestions.
- Try out for school plays and the community theater to get experience performing in front of an audience.

- Attend as many musical performances as possible.
- Get together with friends or classmates and experiment with playing different musical styles.
- If you are interested in writing pop and rock music, read the lyrics of your favorite songs and try to figure out why you like them. Try to write lyrics and put them to music.
- Talk to a musician about his or her career.

music. Advertising for successful groups is usually handled by a record company or promoter.

Very few pop and rock musicians become successful on their recordings alone. Most perform live and gain a following of fans before they make their first recording. For a performance, musicians arrive early to prepare the stage. They set up instruments and sound systems, check sound quality, and become familiar with the stage and facility. The band reviews the list of songs to be performed and it might change the songs based on audience responses. They perform for anywhere from 20 to 30 minutes to several hours. After the concert, they put

Taylor Swift performs for a taping of an MTV show. (Peter Kramer, AP Photo)

their instruments and gear away. Then they head home or, if they are on tour, travel to the next concert location.

Education and Training

It is important to start your music studies as early as possible. You should learn about music theory (the study of how music works), the different types of music, how to play one or more instruments, and how to play with other musicians. Taking English composition and creative writing courses will help you develop your songwriting skills.

A college education isn't necessary for becoming a pop and rock musician, but it can help you learn about music theory and history. You can pursue an education in audio recording, writing, or music at a community college, university, or trade school. Many people also play in bands during their college years. There are also a number of seminars, conferences,

Profile: Taylor Swift (b. 1989)

Taylor Swift is an American country/pop singer, songwriter, and actress. She sharpened her songwriter skills by writing poetry at a young age. She won a national poetry contest while in the fourth grade.

Swift moved on to songwriting, and performed at area contests, fairs, and festivals in her hometown of Wyomissing, Pennsylvania. While performing at the famed Bluebird Café in Nashville, she attracted the attention of a record producer.

Her first song, "Tim McGraw," hit number six on the country charts. Her debut album, *Taylor Swift,* reached the top spot in 2006, eventually staying number one for a record 24 weeks. A string of number one hits from the *Taylor Swift* album followed, earning her the Songwriter/Artist of the Year award from the Nashville Songwriters Association, International.

Swift's second album, *Fearless,* debuted at number one on the Billboard Country charts. The majority of the sales were in digital format, making *Fearless* the best selling digital album in country music history. A single from the *Fearless* album, "Love Story," is considered Swift's signature song, full of elements from the classic story of Romeo and Juliet.

Many of Swift's songs are autobiographical (about her own experiences). She deals with many issues common with her fan base, including love, heartache, friendship, and teenage angst.

She has toured internationally, and has received numerous awards including Country Music Association's Entertainer of the Year, *Billboard* Magazine's Artist of the Year, and an Album of the Year Grammy for *Fearless.* Swift is also credited by the music industry as helping attract a younger audience to country music.

Sources: TaylorSwift.com,
Daily Mail Online

DID YOU KNOW?

The term *rock 'n' roll* was first coined by radio disc jockey Alan Freed in the 1950s. Since then rock music has been an important part of teen culture. Though much of rock music is popular with all ages now, it was the teen culture that evolved in the 1950s that brought the doo wop and boogie woogie music of the South to audiences all across the country. Teens, for the first time in U.S. history, were spending their own money, and they were spending it on the records they heard on the radio. What had previously been music appreciated primarily by African-American audiences, was brought to white audiences by the success of Chuck Berry, Little Richard, Fats Domino, and later, Elvis Presley and Jerry Lee Lewis. Today, there are pop and rock stars of all ethnicities and backgrounds.

and workshops available on songwriting, audio recording, and record producing.

Earnings

When starting out, pop and rock musicians are likely to play clubs and events for free. As they gain fans, they may get a percentage of the club's cover charge or drink receipts in exchange for their performance. The most successful pop and rock musicians can make millions of dollars. According to *Forbes* magazine's "Celebrity 100" ranking of entertainers, U2 ranked the highest of any rock group, with an estimated income of $130 million in 2010. But most musicians earn far less money. The median salary for all full-time musicians and singers was $46,571 in 2010, according to the U.S. Department of Labor.

Outlook

There will always be thousands more rock musicians than there are record contracts. But there always will be opportunities for new performers with record companies and clubs. Record companies are always looking for original sounds and talents.

FOR MORE INFO

Contact the following organizations to learn about the industry and opportunities available to young musicians:

American Federation of Musicians of the United States and Canada
1501 Broadway, Suite 600
New York, NY 10036-5505
212-869-1330
http://www.afm.org

American Guild of Musical Artists
1430 Broadway, 14th Floor
New York, NY 10018-3308
212-265-3687
http://www.musicalartists.org

American Society of Composers, Authors, and Publishers
One Lincoln Plaza
New York, NY 10023-7129
212-621-6000
http://www.ascap.com

To participate in online forums about music education and to read a variety of useful online brochures, such as *Careers in Music* and *How to Nail a College Entrance Audition,* visit the following Web site:
MENC: The National Association for Music Education
1806 Robert Fulton Drive
Reston, VA 20191-4341
800-336-3768
http://www.menc.org

For information on choosing a music school and a database of accredited music schools in the United States, visit the NASM Web site.
National Association of Schools of Music (NASM)
11250 Roger Bacon Drive, Suite 21
Reston, VA 20190-5248
703-437-0700
info@arts-accredit.org
http://nasm.arts-accredit.org

The SGA offers song critiques and workshops in select cities. Visit its Web site for further information on such events.
Songwriters Guild of America (SGA)
5120 Virginia Way, Suite C22
Brentwood, TN 37027-7594
615-742-9945
http://www.songwritersguild.com

This organization offers networking opportunities, career information, and a mentoring program for women in music.
Women In Music
http://womeninmusic.org

Many musicians are using the Internet and social networking sites to reach new fans. They are marketing their music themselves and building a fan base without the help of record companies or reviews in newspapers and magazines.

Screenwriters

What Screenwriters Do

A screenplay details everything that happens in a movie or television show, including dialogue, video and audio instructions, and the movements of the actors. *Screenwriters* write scripts for movies and television shows. The themes may be their own ideas or stories assigned by a producer or director. Often, screenwriters are hired to turn, or adapt, popular plays or novels into screenplays. Writers of original screenplays create their own stories, which are produced for the movie industry or television programs, such as comedies, dramas, documentaries, variety shows, and entertainment specials.

Screenwriters must not only be creative, but they must also have great research skills. For projects such as historical movies, documentaries, and medical or science programs, research is a very important step.

Screenwriters start with an outline, or a treatment, of the story's plot. Scripts are written in a two-column format. One column is used for dialogue and sound, the other for video instructions. One page of script equals about one minute of running time, though it varies. Each page has about 150 words and takes about 20 seconds to read. When the director or producer approves the story outline, screenwriters then complete the story for production. During the writing process, screenwriters write many drafts (versions) of the script. They frequently meet with directors and producers to discuss script changes.

Some screenwriters work alone and others work with a team of writers. Many specialize in certain types of scripts, such as

EXPLORING

- One of the best ways to learn about screenwriting is to read and study scripts. Watch a movie while following the script at the same time.
- Read books about working as a screenwriter. See the Browse and Learn More section for some suggestions.
- Read industry publications. See the Browse and Learn More section for some suggestions.

- There are computer software programs that can help you create a screenplay. Check if they are available at your local or community library.
- Write a play for your classmates or friends to perform. Have a friend who is interested in film video record the performance.
- Talk to a screenwriter about his or her career.

dramas, comedies, and documentaries. *Motion picture screenwriters* usually write alone or with a writing partner and exclusively for movies. Screenwriters for television series work very long hours in the studio. Many television shows have limited runs, so much of the work for television screenwriters is not continuous.

Education and Training

In high school, you should develop your writing skills by taking English, theater, speech, and journalism classes. Social studies and foreign language classes can also be helpful in creating interesting scripts. Other important classes include history, psychology, and computer science.

DID YOU KNOW?

Women screenwriters were much more prominent in the early days of filmmaking. Half of the films made before 1925 were written by women, such as Frances Marion (*Stella Dallas, The Scarlet Letter*) and Anita Loos (*The Women*). Marion was the highest-paid screenwriter from 1916 to the 1930s, and she served as the first vice president of the Writer's Guild. Though a smaller percentage of feature films written by women are produced today, more women screenwriters have won Academy Awards since 1985 than in all the previous years. Among recent Oscar winners are Ruth Prawer Jhabvala (*A Room With a View* and *Howard's End*), Jane Campion (*The Piano*), Callie Khouri (*Thelma and Louise*), Emma Thompson (*Sense and Sensibility*), Sofia Coppola (*Lost in Translation*), and Diablo Cody (*Juno*).

The best way to prepare for a career as a screenwriter is to write and read every day. A college degree is not required, but a liberal arts education is helpful because it exposes you to a wide range of subjects. Some colleges offer degrees in screenwriting or film studies. While in school, become involved in theater to learn about all of the elements required by a screenplay, such as characters, plots, and themes. Book clubs, creative writing classes, and film study are also good ways to learn the basic elements of screenwriting.

Earnings

Annual wages for screenwriters vary widely. Some screenwriters make hundreds of thousands of dollars from their scripts. Others write and film their own scripts without receiving any payment at all, relying on backers and loans. Screenwriters who work independently do not earn regular salaries. They are paid a fee for each script they write. Those who write for ongoing television shows do earn regular salaries. According to the Writers Guild of America (WGA) 2008 Theatrical and Television Basic Agreement, earnings for writers of an original screenplay ranged from $62,642 to $117,602 during the 2010-11 segment of the contract. The U.S. Department of Labor reports that writers employed in the movie industry had mean annual earnings of $78,680 in 2010. Television writers earned $66,110 a year, on average.

The Oscar Goes To. . .

The following screenwriters were Oscar winners for best original screenplay:

2010: David Seidler for *The King's Speech*
2009: Mark Boal for *The Hurt Locker*
2008: Dustin Lance Black for *Milk*
2007: Diablo Cody for *Juno*
2006: Michael Arndt for *Little Miss Sunshine*

For more information on Academy Award-winning films, visit http://www.oscars.org/awardsdatabase.

Outlook

It will be hard to land a job as a screenwriter because so many people are attracted to the field. In this industry, it is helpful to network and make contacts. If you want to be a screenwriter, it is important to work hard to break into the field and never stop following your dreams. On the brighter side, the growth of the cable industry has increased demand for original screenplays and adaptations. Additionally, people in foreign countries are increasingly interested in watching American movies. These developments should create more demand for screenwriters.

FOR MORE INFO

To learn more about screenwriting, contact
Writers Guild of America (WGA)
East Chapter
250 Hudson Street
New York, NY 10013-1413
212-767-7800
http://www.wgaeast.org

Writers Guild of America (WGA)
West Chapter
7000 West Third Street
Los Angeles, CA 90048-4329
800-548-4532
http://www.wga.org

Singers

EXPLORING

- Join music clubs at school and sing in choirs or ensembles.
- Many singers get their start singing in their church or synagogue at an early age.
- Take part in school drama productions that involve musical numbers.
- Audition for roles in community musical productions.
- Participate in summer programs that will help you improve your music skills.
- Watch a singer at a school or community concert.
- Talk to a singer about his or her career.

What Singers Do

Singers are musicians whose instruments are their voices. They use their knowledge of musical tone, phrasing, harmony, and melody to create vocal music. Singers are also known as *vocalists*.

Singers are classified in two ways. The first way is by the range of their voices. Sopranos have the highest voices, followed by mezzo-sopranos, contraltos (or altos), tenors, baritones, and basses, who have the lowest voices. The second way that singers may be classified is by the type, or genre, of music they sing, such as classical, rock, folk, opera, jazz, or country.

Nearly all singers work with instrumental musicians. A singer's backup group may be as small as one piano player or a single guitarist or as large as a full symphony orchestra. In between are jazz combos, dance bands, and rock bands. Singers also work in choirs, barbershop quartets, and other singing groups, with or without accompaniment.

The Jonas Brothers perform in concert. (Jennifer Graylock, AP Photo)

Many singers travel throughout the country and even the world to perform live for audiences. Some singers, especially those who sing classical music, sing in more than one language. Operas, for example, are often written in Italian, French, and German, so singers must be able to pronounce and understand the lyrics. Some singers are primarily *studio singers*. That is, they rarely perform in front of audiences but instead record their singing in sound studios. They may record television and radio commercials, or perform songs for CDs or Internet download.

Singers can also be actors. Musical plays on the stage require singers with strong voices who can also act well. Actors who can sing will find more job opportunities in the theater if they can dance as well.

Education and Training

Most singers begin learning their skills at an early age. Young children can sing in school or church choirs. Students can join concert choirs or take part in musical plays.

Most professional singers have singing teachers and voice coaches. They practice vocal exercises every day, such as scales and intervals, breath control, and diction exercises to increase the range, power, and clarity of their voices. Some

Words to Learn

breath control the ability to use one's abdominal muscles to regulate one's breathing while singing

harmony a combination of musical notes mixed with intervals and chords

interval in music, the distance between two pitches

lyrics the words of a song

melody a succession of single pitches or tones

phrasing the manner in which lyrics in a musical composition are presented by a singer

pitch the lowness or highness of a tone

rhythm the organized movement of a musical composition over time

scale a particular set of notes arranged in an ascending or descending order

tempo Italian for speed; the speed at which a piece of music is played or sung

timbre the particular quality of sound of a voice or instrument

timing in music, the proper spacing between various musical elements

tone a sound of a particular pitch

Source: Essentials of Music.com

Fame & Fortune: Justin Bieber (b. 1994)

Justin Bieber is a Canadian pop/R&B singer. Unlike the other teen stars of his generation, Bieber did not become popular by appearing on cable television channels such Disney or Nickelodeon. Instead, he used the Internet to publicize his talents.

After participating in an area talent show at age 12, Bieber's mother posted a video of the performance on the video-sharing site YouTube for relatives and friends to enjoy. More performance videos were added and Bieber's YouTube following grew, largely by word of mouth.

As fate would have it, one of Bieber's videos was accidentally viewed by Scooter Braun, an executive at So So Def Recordings, a record label. Impressed by what he saw, Braun brought the teenager to meet with R&B singer, Usher, who ultimately helped Bieber win a recording contract with Island Records. Braun also helped build Bieber's popularity and marketability by continuing to shoot and upload new music videos on YouTube, as well as giving him a Twitter account.

Under Usher's guidance, Bieber released his first album, *My World,* in 2009. Two singles from this album, "One Time" and "Baby," became platinum hits internationally. He released two digital singles, "Never Let You Go" and "U Smile," both of which reached the top 30 of the U.S. Hot 100 list.

Bieber tours internationally and makes regular mall appearances, many times drawing masses of teens. He has performed during many music award shows and benefits, as well as for President Obama and his family.

Sources: Justinbiebermusic.com, *New York Times,* Billboard.com

colleges and universities offer music degrees with a concentration in voice.

Earnings

Full-time singers had yearly earnings that ranged from less than $18,000 to more than $124,000 in 2010, according to the U.S.

FOR MORE INFO

Contact these organizations to learn about the industry and opportunities available to young musicians.

American Federation of Musicians of the United States and Canada
1501 Broadway, Suite 600
New York, NY 10036-5505
212-869-1330
http://www.afm.org

American Guild of Musical Artists
1430 Broadway, 14th Floor
New York, NY 10018-3308
212-265-3687
http://www.musicalartists.org

American Society of Composers, Authors, and Publishers
One Lincoln Plaza
New York, NY 10023-7129
212-621-6000
http://www.ascap.com

Visit the BMI Web site to learn more about performing rights, music publishing, copyright, and the business of songwriting.

Broadcast Music Inc. (BMI)
3340 Peachtree Road, NE, Suite 570
Atlanta, GA 30326-1059
404-261-5151
http://www.bmi.com

To participate in online forums about music education and to read a variety of useful online brochures, such as *Careers in Music* and *How to Nail a College Entrance Audition*, visit the following Web site:

MENC: The National Association for Music Education
1806 Robert Fulton Drive
Reston, VA 20191-4341
800-336-3768
http://www.menc.org

For information on choosing a music school and a database of accredited music schools in the United States, visit the NASM Web site.

National Association of Schools of Music (NASM)
11250 Roger Bacon Drive, Suite 21
Reston, VA 20190-5248
703-437-0700
info@arts-accredit.org
http://nasm.arts-accredit.org

The SGA offers song critiques and other workshops in select cities. Visit its Web site for further information on such events.

Songwriters Guild of America (SGA)
5120 Virginia Way, Suite C22
Brentwood, TN 37027-7594
615-742-9945
http://www.songwritersguild.com

This organization offers networking opportunities, career information, and a mentoring program for women in music.

Women In Music
http://womeninmusic.org

Department of Labor. Many singers only work part time and earn less than $5,000 a year.

A singer in a dance club or nightclub can earn $150 to $355 per performance, according to MENC: The National Association for Music Education. Members of concert or opera choruses earn $100 or more for a performance. Concert soloists receive $450 or more for each performance, while opera soloists make $1,100 or more per performance.

Many singers supplement their earnings by working at other positions, such as teaching at schools or giving private lessons.

Outlook

There always has been strong competition for the limited number of job opportunities for singers. Usually only the most talented will find regular employment. Because most singers only find part-time job opportunities, it is best for aspiring singers to also consider music-related jobs that will provide a steady income. Employment in composition, education, broadcasting, music therapy, or community arts management is far more secure.

Songwriters

What Songwriters Do

Songwriters write the words and sometimes the music for songs, including songs for recordings, advertising jingles, and theatrical performances. They may also perform these songs. Songwriters who write only the words and not the music are called *lyricists*.

Songwriters may choose to write about emotions, such as love, happiness, or sadness. They put their ideas into a small number of words, focusing on the sounds of the words together. Many songwriters carry a notebook and write about things that they hear or see. Others use computers to record their thoughts. They may write songs about people, events, or experiences. They may write about broad themes that will be understood by everyone. They get ideas from current events or social situations such as poverty, racial issues, or war. Or they may write about personal issues, based on their own experiences or conversations with others.

Songwriters usually have a musical style in mind when they write lyrics. These styles include pop, rock, hip hop, rap, country, blues, jazz, and classical.

Songwriters who work for advertising agencies have to write about certain products for radio and television commercials. Producers also hire songwriters to write lyrics for opera, movies, or Broadway shows (Broadway is the name given to the main theater district in New York City).

Many songwriters have a certain method for writing songs. Sometimes, they write the title first because it allows them to capture a theme in just a few words. The first words of the song are often the strongest, to get the attention of the listener. Many songwriters find that there are about four common characteristics found in a song: an identifiable, universal idea; a memorable title; a strong beginning; and an appropriate form, including rhythm, verse, and refrain.

Lyricists who do not write music work with a composer. The composer might play a few measures on an instrument and the lyricist tries to write words that fit well with the music. Or, the lyricist suggests a few words or lines and the composer tries to write music that fits the words. Each partner must trust the other's talent and be able to work together to create a full song.

Education and Training

Songwriters must have a good understanding of language and grammar. In high school, you should take courses in English composition, poetry, music theory, and journalism. Learning how to play a musical instrument is a good idea. You also should take classes in musical composition.

There is really no formal training that a songwriter must have in order to write songs. Musical training is important, though. Songwriting workshops often are offered by community colleges and music schools. College music programs teach you how to read music and understand harmony. They also expose you to a variety of musical styles.

Earnings

Songwriters' earnings vary from almost nothing to many millions of dollars. A songwriter may write songs for several years before actually selling or recording a song. Songwriters receive royalties (payments) if their songs are played on the radio, in movies and on television shows, at sporting events, or in other settings. Royalties from a song may reach $20,000 per year or more for each song. A successful songwriter may earn $100,000 or more a year from the royalties of several songs.

Tips for Success

To be a successful songwriter, you should

- be creative
- have a good imagination
- be familiar with many different musical styles
- have a working knowledge of musical instruments, especially the piano
- have a love of words and music
- be able to accept constructive criticism regarding your talents
- be ambitious

Outlook

Songwriters find much competition in their field. It may take years of writing and submitting your songs to earn a reputation and become successful. On the other hand, you may be very talented, but never get that big break that allows you to have a full-time career as a songwriter. Songwriters should find more opportunities outside of the recording industry, writing music for television, multimedia projects, advertising, and the Internet.

FOR MORE INFO

Contact these organizations to learn about the industry and opportunities available to young musicians.

American Federation of Musicians of the United States and Canada
1501 Broadway, Suite 600
New York, NY 10036-5505
212-869-1330
http://www.afm.org

American Society of Composers, Authors, and Publishers
One Lincoln Plaza
New York, NY 10023-7129
212-621-6000
http://www.ascap.com

Visit the BMI Web site to learn more about performing rights, music publishing, copyright, and the business of songwriting.

Broadcast Music Inc. (BMI)
3340 Peachtree Road, NE, Suite 570
Atlanta, GA 30326-1059
404-261-5151
http://www.bmi.com

To participate in online forums about music education and to read a variety of useful online brochures, such as *Careers in Music* and *How to Nail a College Entrance Audition*, visit the following Web site:

MENC: The National Association for Music Education
1806 Robert Fulton Drive
Reston, VA 20191-4341

800-336-3768
http://www.menc.org

For information on choosing a music school and a database of accredited music schools in the United States, visit the NASM Web site.

National Association of Schools of Music (NASM)
11250 Roger Bacon Drive, Suite 21
Reston, VA 20190-5248
703-437-0700
info@arts-accredit.org
http://nasm.arts-accredit.org

The society represents composers, lyricists, and songwriters who work in film, television, and multimedia. Visit its Web site for career resources, an online hall of fame, and information on *The SCORE*, its quarterly publication.

Society of Composers & Lyricists
8447 Wilshire Boulevard, Suite 401
Beverly Hills CA 90211-3209
310-281-2812
http://www.thescl.com

The SGA offers song critiques and workshops in select cities. Visit its Web site for more information on such events.

Songwriters Guild of America (SGA)
5120 Virginia Way, Suite C22
Brentwood, TN 37027-7594
615-742-9945
http://www.songwritersguild.com

Stage Production Technicians

What Stage Production Technicians Do

Stage production technicians install lights, sound equipment, and scenery for theater stages. They build the stages for theatrical and musical events in parks, stadiums, and other places. For small productions, stage workers must be able to do a variety of tasks. For larger productions, such as those on Broadway (the main theater district in New York City), stage technicians may be responsible for only one or two tasks. There are many different types of stage production technicians. They can be carpenters, prop makers, lighting designers, lighting-equipment operators, sound technicians, electricians, and riggers (who set up and maintain ropes and chains used to move props, actors, and sets during theater productions).

Stage technicians use drawings of the stage and written instructions from the stage designer. They talk to the stage manager to decide what kinds of sets, scenery, props, lighting, and sound equipment are needed. Then they collect or build the props or scenery, using hammers, saws, and other hand

EXPLORING

- Read books about theater productions. See the Browse and Learn More section for some suggestions.
- Participate in school theatrical performances.
- Volunteer to do behind-the-scenes work for amateur community theater productions or special benefit events.
- Talk to a stage production technician about his or her career.

and power tools. Stage technicians position lights and sound equipment on or around the stage. They clamp light fixtures to supports and connect electrical wiring from the fixtures to power sources and control panels. During rehearsals and performances, stage technicians pull ropes and cables that raise and lower curtains and other equipment. Sometimes they also operate the lighting and sound equipment.

Stage production technicians work for theatre, music, dance, and other performing arts companies. Other employers include casinos, amusement parks, cruise ships, arenas, and auditoriums.

> **DID YOU KNOW?**
>
> In 2008:
> - Approximately 32 million people attended a nonprofit theatre production in the United States.
> - Sixty-three percent of theatre workers had artistic jobs, 26 percent had technical positions, and 11 percent had managerial jobs.
> - There were 1,919 nonprofit, professional theatres in the United States.
>
> Source: Theater Communications Group

Education and Training

Stage production technicians must be high school graduates. Many employers prefer to hire stage technicians who are graduates of two-year junior or community colleges. If you are interested in stage production work you should make sure to take courses in math, English, drama, and history. Carpentry or electronics courses that include work with lighting and sound will be helpful. Participate in the various parts of school theatrical performances, from acting to working on sets to helping with promotion.

Earnings

Most stage technicians earn between $25,000 and $40,000 a year. Salaries depend on the employer, geographic location, and the technician's responsibilities.

Stage technicians who are hired for their skills as carpenters, electricians, or sound or light technicians earn salaries roughly

Let There Be Light

Lighting equipment and operation is one of the more complex parts of stage production. Following are some lighting terms to know:

fader controls the output level of a lantern (lamp)

floodlights lights that give a general, fixed spread of light

follow spot light directed at actor that can follow all movements

footlights lights set into the stage floor that throw strong general light into the performers' faces

gel colored medium inserted in front of the light to change the color of a beam

ghost a beam of light that leaks from a light and falls where it is not wanted

gobo a screen placed in front of a stage light to cast a particular image on stage; also a cut-out shape that is projected

iris a device within a lantern that allows a technician to change the size of a circular beam

equal to the salaries they would receive elsewhere, which range from $15,000 to $80,000 a year.

Outlook

When the economy is strong, employment opportunities for stage production technicians are generally good. When the economy is weak, fewer people attend plays and other entertainment events, which creates less demand for technicians. People who can do a variety of tasks stand the best chance of employment. For example, someone who knows about both sound systems and lighting is more likely to get a good position in theater. Employment opportunities will be best in large cities that have a large number of theatres.

FOR MORE INFO

For information on union membership, contact
International Alliance of Theatrical Stage Employees, Moving Picture Technicians, Artists and Allied Crafts
1430 Broadway, 20th Floor
New York, NY 10018-3348
212-730-1770
http://www.iatse-intl.org

For information about opportunities in nonprofit theaters, contact
Theatre Communications Group
520 Eighth Avenue, 24th Floor
New York, NY 10018-4156
212-609-5900
tcg@tcg.org
http://www.tcg.org

Stunt Performers

What Stunt Performers Do

Stunt performers work on film and television scenes that are risky and dangerous. They act out car crashes and chases. They participate in mock fist and sword fights. They actually fall from cars, motorcycles, horses, and buildings. They perform airplane and helicopter gags, ride through raging river rapids, and face wild animals, such as bulls, bears, and buffaloes. Some stunt performers focus on just one type of stunt.

There are two general types of stunt roles: *double* and *nondescript.* The first requires a stunt performer to double, or take the place of, a star actor in a dangerous scene. As a double, the stunt performer must portray the character in the same way as the star actor.

In a nondescript role, the stunt performer does not stand in for another actor, but plays an incidental character in a dangerous scene. An example of a nondescript role is a driver in a freeway chase scene. Stunt performers occasionally have speaking parts.

The idea for a stunt usually begins with the *screenwriter,* the person who writes the script for the movie or TV show. Once the stunts are written into the script, it is the job of the *director* (who oversees the entire movie or TV show) to decide how they will appear on the screen. Directors, especially of large, action-filled movies, often seek the help of a *stunt coordinator.* A stunt coordinator can quickly decide if a stunt is possible and what is the best and safest way to perform it. Stunt coordinators plan the stunt. They also oversee the setup and construction of

EXPLORING

- Read books about the work of stunt performers. See the Browse and Learn More section for some suggestions.
- Stunt performers must be in top physical shape and train like athletes. To develop your physical strength and coordination, play on sports teams and participate in school athletics.
- Acting in school or religious plays can teach you about taking direction.
- Theme parks and circuses use stunt performers. Visit these places and try to meet the performers after shows.
- Talk to a stunt performer about his or her career.

special sets and materials and either hire or recommend the most qualified stunt performer.

Although a stunt may last only a few seconds in a movie or television show, it can take several hours or even days to prepare for the stunt. Stunt performers work with props, makeup, wardrobe, and set design departments. They also work closely with the special and visual effects team. A carefully planned stunt can often be completed in just one take. It is more common for the stunt person to perform the stunt several times until the director is happy with the performance.

Stunt work can be very dangerous. Stunt performers do many things to make sure that they are safe during filming. They use air bags, body pads, or cables in stunts involving falls or crashes. If a stunt performer must enter a burning building, he or she wears special fireproof clothing and protective cream on the skin.

DID YOU KNOW?

Women daredevils in the 19th century drew as many spectators as the men.

Signora Josephine Girardelli was known as the "Fire-Proof Lady." She earned that title by holding boiling oil in her mouth and hands and performing other feats of stamina.

Bess Houdini assisted her husband Harry in many famous tricks, including one which ended with her tied up and sealed in a trunk.

May Wirth was a talented equestrian (horse rider), known as "The Wonder Rider of the World" for her somersaults and other stunts while riding a rushing horse.

Even amateurs got into the act. Annie Taylor, a 63-year-old Michigan school-teacher, became the first person to go over the Niagara Falls in a barrel.

Education and Training

No standard training exists for stunt performers. They usually start out by contacting stunt coordinators and asking for work. If the stunt coordinator thinks the person has the proper credentials, he or she will be hired for basic stunt work like fight scenes. A number of stunt schools, such as the United Stuntmen's Association International Stunt School, offer training to people who want to become stunt performers.

Stunt performers get a lot of training on the job. Every new type of stunt has its own challenges. By working closely with stunt coordinators, performers learn how to eliminate most of the risks involved in stunts. Even so, injuries are very common among stunt performers. There is even the possibility of death during very dangerous stunts.

Earnings

Stunt performers earn the same day rate as other actors, plus extra pay for more difficult and dangerous stunts. Stunt performers must belong to the actor's union, the Screen Actor's Guild (SAG). The SAG minimum day rate for stunt performers was $809 in 2010. Though this may seem like a lot of money, few stunt performers work every day. According to the SAG, the majority of its members make less than $7,500 a year. But those who are in high demand can receive salaries of well over $100,000 a year.

Outlook

There are more than 7,700 stunt performers who belong to the SAG, but only a small number work full time. It's difficult for

Famous Daredevils

Stunt performers have been around much longer than the film industry. Throughout the 19th century, circus performers leaped from buildings, walked tight-ropes, swallowed swords, and stuffed themselves into tiny boxes.

Harry Houdini is one of the most famous showmen in entertainment history. He became internationally famous by escaping in less than a minute from a chain-wrapped crate that was lowered into New York's East River.

Another daredevil was Samuel Gilbert Scott, who showed "extraordinary and surpassing powers in the art of leaping and diving." After swinging about a ship's riggings (ropes and other equipment used to control masts and sails) or jumping from a 240-foot cliff, he'd pass around a hat for donations from fans. His final stunt took place at Waterloo Bridge. While performing predive acrobatics with a rope around his neck, he slipped and strangled to death.

FOR MORE INFO

For more information on earnings and union membership, contact
Screen Actors Guild
5757 Wilshire Boulevard, 7th Floor
Los Angeles, CA 90036-3600
323-954-1600
http://www.sag.com

For information on opportunities in the industry, contact the following organizations:
Stuntmen's Association of Motion Pictures
5200 Lankersheim Boulevard, Suite 190
North Hollywood, CA 91601-3100
818-766-4334
hq@stuntmen.com
http://www.stuntmen.com

Stuntwomen's Association of Motion Pictures
818-762-0907
http://www.stuntwomen.com

For information about the USA training program and images of stunt performers in action, visit the association's Web site.
United Stuntmens Association (USA)
10924 Mukilteo Speedway, PMB 272
Mukilteo, WA 98275-5022
425-645-9552
iboushey@gmail.com
http://www.stuntschool.com

new stunt performers to break into the business. The future of this career may be affected by computer technology. Moviemakers today use special effects and computer-generated imagery for action sequences. Computer-generated stunts are also safer. Safety on film sets has always been a major concern since many stunts are very dangerous. However, using live stunt performers can make a scene seem more real, so talented stunt performers will always be in demand.

Glossary

accredited   approved as meeting established standards for providing good training and education; this approval is usually given by an independent organization of professionals

annual salary   the money an individual earns for an entire year of work

apprentice   a person who is learning a trade by working under the supervision of a skilled worker; apprentices often receive classroom instruction in addition to their supervised practical experience

associate's degree   an academic rank or title granted by a community or junior college or similar institution to graduates of a two-year program of education beyond high school

bachelor's degree   an academic rank or title given to a person who has completed a four-year program of study at a college or university; also called an **undergraduate degree** or baccalaureate

bonus   an award of money in addition to one's typical salary that is given to an employee for extra-special work or achievement on the job

career   an occupation for which a worker receives training and has an opportunity for advancement

certified   approved as meeting established requirements for skill, knowledge, and experience in a particular field; people are certified by an organization of professionals in their field

college   a higher education institution that is above the high school level

community college   a public or private two-year college attended by students who do not usually live at the college; graduates of a community college receive an associate's degree and may transfer to a four-year college or university to complete a bachelor's degree

diploma   a certificate or document given by a school to show that a person has completed a course or has graduated from the school

distance education   a type of educational program that allows students to take classes and complete their education by mail or the Internet

doctorate   the highest academic rank or title granted by a graduate school to a person who has completed a two- to three-year program after having received a master's degree

fellowship   a financial award given for research projects or dissertation assistance; fellowships are commonly offered at the graduate, postgraduate, or doctoral levels

freelancer   a worker who is not a regular employee of a company; they work for themselves and do not receive a regular paycheck

fringe benefit   a payment or benefit to an employee in addition to regular wages or salary; examples of fringe benefits include a pension, a paid vacation, and health or life insurance

graduate school   a school that people may attend after they have received their bachelor's degree; people who complete an educational program at a graduate school earn a master's degree or a doctorate

intern   an advanced student (usually one with at least some college training) in a professional field who is employed in a job that is intended to provide supervised practical experience for the student

internship   1. the position or job of an intern; 2. the period of time when a person is an intern

junior college   a two-year college that offers courses like those in the first half of a four-year college program; graduates of a junior college usually receive an associate's degree and may transfer to a four-year college or university to complete a bachelor's degree

liberal arts   the subjects covered by college courses that develop broad general knowledge rather than specific occupational skills; the liberal arts are often considered to include philosophy, literature and the arts, history, language, and some courses in the social sciences and natural sciences

major (in college)   the academic field in which a student specializes and receives a degree

master's degree   an academic rank or title granted by a graduate school to a person who has completed a one- or two-year program after having received a bachelor's degree

pension   an amount of money paid regularly by an employer to a former employee after he or she retires from working

scholarship   a gift of money to a student to help the student pay for further education

social studies   courses of study (such as civics, geography, and history) that deal with how human societies work

starting salary   salary paid to a newly hired employee; the starting salary is usually a smaller amount than is paid to a more experienced worker

technical college   a private or public college offering two- or four-year programs in technical subjects; technical colleges offer courses in both general and technical subjects and award associate's degrees and bachelor's degrees

undergraduate   a student at a college or university who has not yet received a degree

undergraduate degree   see **bachelor's degree**

union   an organization whose members are workers in a particular industry or company; the union works to gain better wages, benefits, and working conditions for its members; also called a labor union or trade union

vocational school   a public or private school that offers training in one or more skills or trades

wage   money that is paid in return for work done, especially money paid on the basis of the number of hours or days worked

Browse and Learn More

Books

Albert, Lisa Rondinelli. *So You Want to Be a Film or TV Actor?* Berkeley Heights, N.J.: Enslow Publishers, 2008.

Allen, Laurie. *Sixty Comedy Duet Scenes for Teens: Real-Life Situations for Laughter.* Colorado Springs, Colo.: Meriwether Publishing, 2008.

Barber, Nicola. *Should I Play the Flute?* Chicago: Heinemann-Raintree, 2007.

Belli, Mary Lou, and Dinah Lenney. *Acting for Young Actors: The Ultimate Teen Guide.* New York: Back Stage Books, 2006.

Boughn, Jenn. *Stage Combat: Fisticuffs, Stunts, and Swordplay for Theater and Film.* New York: Allworth Press, 2006.

Buckland, Gail. *Who Shot Rock and Roll: A Photographic History, 1955-Present.* New York: Knopf, 2009.

Buckley, Annie. *Making Movies.* Mankato, Minn.: The Child's World, 2006.

———. *Movies.* Ann Arbor, Mich.: Cherry Lake Publishing, 2008.

D'Cruz, Anna-Marie. *Make Your Own Musical Instruments.* New York: PowerKids Press, 2009.

Desjardins, Christian, and Christopher Young. *Inside Film Music: Composers Speak.* Los Angeles: Silman-James Press, 2007.

Dunkleberger, Amy. *So You Want to Be a Film or TV Director?* Berkeley Heights, N.J.: Enslow Publishers, 2007.

———. *So You Want to Be a Film or TV Screenwriter?* Berkeley Heights, N.J.: Enslow Publishers, 2007.

Dunn, Mary R. *I Want to Make Movies.* New York: PowerKids Press, 2008.

Fishkin, Rebecca. *Dance; A Practical Guide to Pursuing the Art.* Mankato, Minn.: Compass Point Books, 2010.

Franks, Katie. *I Want to Be a Movie Star.* New York: PowerKids Press, 2007.

Frederick, Robin. *Shortcuts to Hit Songwriting: 126 Proven Techniques for Writing Songs That Sell.* Calabasas, Calif.: Taxi Music Books, 2008.

Hamlett, Christina. *Screenwriting for Teens: The 100 Principles of Screenwriting Every Budding Writer Must Know.* Studio City, Calif.: Michael Wiese Productions, 2006.

Heatley, Michael, and Scotty Moore. *The Definitive Encyclopedia of Rock.* London, U.K.: Flame Tree Publishing, 2007.

Helsby, Genevieve. *Those Amazing Musical Instruments! with CD: Your Guide to the Orchestra Through Sounds and Stories.* Naperville, Ill.: Sourcebooks, 2007.

Holtz, Martina. *Voggy's ABC of Music: Basic Music Theory for Kids.* Wachtberg-Villip, Germany: Voggenreiter, 2005.

Hopper, Jessica. *The Girls' Guide to Rocking: How to Start a Band, Book Gigs, and Get Rolling to Rock Stardom.* New York: Workman Publishing Company, 2009.

Horn, Geoffrey M. *Movie Acting.* New York: Gareth Stevens Publishing, 2006.

———. *Movie Stunts and Special Effects.* New York: Gareth Stevens Publishing, 2006.

———. *Writing, Producing, and Directing Movies.* New York: Gareth Stevens Publishing, 2006.

Houston, Scott. *Play Piano in a Flash for Kids!: A Fun and Easy Way for Kids to Start Playing the Piano.* New York: Hyperion, 2006.

Jay, Joshua. *Magic: The Complete Course.* New York: Workman Publishing Company, 2008.

Kallen, Stuart A. *Instruments of Music.* Farmington Hills, Mich.: Lucent Books, 2006.

Knight, M. J. *Brass and Woodwinds.* Mankato, Minn.: Smart Apple Media, 2005.

———. *Flutes.* Mankato, Minn.: Smart Apple Media, 2005.

———. *Keyboards.* Mankato, Minn.: Smart Apple Media, 2005.

———. *Percussion.* Mankato, Minn.: Smart Apple Media, 2005.

———. *Stringed Instruments.* Mankato, Minn.: Smart Apple Media, 2005.

Lanier, Troy, and Clay Nichols. *Filmmaking for Teens: Pulling Off Your Shorts.* 2nd ed. Studio City, Calif.: Michael Wiese Productions, 2010.

Luboff, Pete, and Pat Luboff. *101 Songwriting Wrongs and How to Right Them.* 2nd ed. Cincinnati, Ohio: Writers Digest Books, 2007.

Mayfield, Katherine. *Acting A to Z: The Young Person's Guide to a Stage or Screen Career.* New York: Back Stage Books, 2007.

Metzler, Bo. *What We Do: Working in the Theatre.* West Conshohocken, Penn.: Infinity Publishing, 2008.

Miles, Liz. *The Orchestra.* Chicago: Heinemann-Raintree, 2009.

Nathan, Amy. *Meet the Dancers: From Ballet, Broadway, and Beyond.* New York: Henry Holt and Co., 2008.

O'Brien, Lisa, and Stephen MacEachern. *Lights, Camera, Action!: Making Movies and TV From the Inside Out.* Toronto, ON, Canada: Maple Tree Press, 2007.

O'Neill, Joseph. *Movie Director.* Ann Arbor, Mich.: Cherry Lake Publishing, 2009.

Phillpotts, James. *Should I Play the Trumpet?* Chicago: Heinemann-Raintree, 2007.

Pinkerton, Judith P., and Barbara Kiwak. *Bold Composer: A Story About Ludwig Van Beethoven.* Minneapolis: Millbrook Press, 2006.

Rock 'n' Roll Camp for Girls, and Carrie Brownstein. *Rock 'n' Roll Camp for Girls: How to Start a Band, Write Songs, Record an Album, and Rock Out!* San Francisco: Chronicle Books, 2008.

Rudow, Barbara. *Bold Moves: A Dancer's Journey.* La Jolla, Calif.: Scobre Press, 2009.

Schumacher, Thomas, and Jeff Kurtti. *How Does the Show Go On: An Introduction to the Theater.* New York: Disney Editions, 2007.

Seskin, Steve. Eve Aldridge, Shino Arihara, Bob Barner, et al. *Sing My Song: A Kid's Guide to Songwriting.* New York: Tricycle Press, 2008.

Sherman, Pat. *The Secret, Mystifying, Unusual History of Magic.* Mankato, Minn.: Capstone Press, 2010.

Skog, Jason. *Acting; A Practical Guide to Pursuing the Art.* Mankato, Minn.: Compass Point Books, 2010.

———. *Screenwriting; A Practical Guide to Pursuing the Art.* Mankato, Minn.: Compass Point Books, 2010.

Spilsbury, Richard. *Should I Play the Clarinet?* Chicago: Heinemann-Raintree, 2007.

———. *Should I Play the Guitar?* Chicago: Heinemann-Raintree, 2007.

———. *Should I Play the Violin?* Chicago: Heinemann-Raintree, 2007.

Townsend, Charles Barry. *World's Greatest Magic Tricks.* New York: Sterling Publishing Company, 2005.

Tremaine, Jon. *Amazing Card Tricks.* Hauppauge, N.Y.: Barron's Educational Series, 2007.

Periodicals

American Theatre
http://www.tcg.org

Cinefex
http://www.cinefex.com

Dance Magazine
http://www.dancemagazine.com

The Hollywood Reporter
http://www.hollywoodreporter.com

Plays
http://playsmagazine.com

Screen Actor
http://www.sag.org/screenactor

Time for Kids
http://www.timeforkids.com/TFK

Variety
http://www.variety.com

Web Sites

About.com: Radio
http://radio.about.com

Academy of Motion Picture Arts and Sciences
http://www.oscars.org

Acting Workshop On-Line: So You Want to be an Actor
http://www.redbirdstudio.com/AWOL/acting2.html

AMC Filmsite
http://www.filmsite.org

American Film Institute
http://www.afi.com

American Library Association: Great Web Sites for Kids
http://www.ala.org/greatsites

The Austin Symphony Kids
http://austinsymphonykids.org

Baltimore Symphony Orchestra Kids
http://www.bsomusic.org/bsokids

Children's Creative Theater Guide
http://library.thinkquest.org/5291

Dallas Symphony Orchestra: Kids
http://www.dsokids.com

The Internet Movie Database
http://us.imdb.com

John Philip Sousa: American Conductor, Composer & Patriot
http://www.dws.org/sousa

National Academy of Television Arts & Sciences
http://www.emmyonline.tv

New York City Ballet: Kids and Families
http://www.nycballet.com/families/families.html

Radio Hall of Fame
http://www.radiohof.org

Ringling Bros. and Barnum & Bailey Circus
http://www.ringling.com

San Francisco Symphony Kids' Site
http://www.sfskids.org

Welcome to the Ballet
http://library.thinkquest.org/21702

Index